MASTERING MICHIGAN'S HIGH SCHOOL TEST IN SOCIAL STUDIES

JAMES KILLORAN

STUART ZIMMER

MARK JARRETT

 JARRETT PUBLISHING COMPANY

East Coast:
19 Cross Street
Ronkonkoma, NY 11779
(516) 981-4248

West Coast:
10 Folin Lane
Lafayette, CA 94549
(925) 906-9742

1-800-859-7679   FAX: (516) 588-4722

www.jarrettpub.com

Jarrett Publishing Company
19 Cross Street
Ronkonkoma, New York 11779

ISBN 1-882422-43-0

First Edition
Printed in the United States of America
by Malloy Lithographing, Inc., Ann Arbor, Michigan

10   9   8   7   6   5   4   3   2   1   02   01   00   99

ABOUT THE AUTHORS

James Killoran is a retired Assistant Principal. He has written *Government and You* and *Economics and You*. Mr. Killoran has extensive experience in test writing for the New York State Board of Regents in social studies and has served on the Committee for Testing of the National Council of Social Studies. His article on social studies testing has been published in *Social Education*, the country's leading social studies journal. In addition, Mr. Killoran has won a number of awards for outstanding teaching and curriculum development, including, "Outstanding Social Studies Teacher" and "Outstanding Social Studies Supervisor" in New York City. In 1993, he was awarded an Advanced Certificate for Teachers of Social Studies by the N.C.S.S.

Stuart Zimmer is a retired social studies teacher. He has written *Government and You* and *Economics and You*. He served as a test writer for the New York State Board of Regents in social studies and has written for the National Merit Scholarship Examination. In addition, he has published numerous articles on teaching and testing in social studies journals. He has presented many demonstrations and educational workshops at state and national teachers' conferences. In 1989, Mr. Zimmer's achievements were recognized by the New York State Legislature with a Special Legislative Resolution passed in his honor.

Mark Jarrett is a former social studies teacher and a practicing attorney at the San Francisco office of Baker and McKenzie, the world's largest law firm. Mr. Jarrett has served as a test writer for the New York State Board of Regents in social studies and has taught at Hofstra University. He was educated at Columbia University, the London School of Economics, the Law School of the University of California at Berkeley, and Stanford University, where he is a doctoral candidate in history. Mr. Jarrett has received several academic awards, including Order of the Coif at Berkeley and the David and Christina Phelps Harris Fellowship at Stanford University.

ALSO BY KILLORAN, ZIMMER AND JARRETT

Michigan: Its Land and Its People
Making Connections: Michigan and the Wider World
Mastering the Social Studies MEAP Test: Grade 5
Mastering the Social Studies MEAP Test: Grade 8
The Key to Understanding Global History
The Key to Understanding U.S. History and Government
Mastering Global Studies
Mastering U.S. History and Government
Mastering Ohio's 9th Grade Citizenship Test
Mastering Ohio's 12th Grade Citizenship Test
Los Estados Unidos: su historia, su gobierno
Nuestro mundo: su historia, sus culturas
Ohio: Its Land and Its People
Ohio: Its Neighbors, Near and Far
Principios de economía
Texas: Its Land and Its People
New York: Its Land and Its People
North Carolina: The Tar Heel State

ACKNOWLEDGMENTS

The authors would like to thank the following Michigan educators who reviewed the manuscript, and whose comments, suggestions and recommendations proved invaluable:

Michael Yocum
Executive Director, Michigan Council for the Social Studies
Consultant to the Oakland County School District

David Harris
Social Studies Consultant
Oakland School District
Oakland County, Michigan

Layout and typesetting by Maple Hill Press, Ltd., Huntington, NY
Maps and graphics by Morris Kantor and Computerized Cartography

This book is dedicated
...to my wife Donna and my children Christian, Carrie, and Jesse — *James Killoran*
...to my wife Joan and my children Todd and Ronald — *Stuart Zimmer*
...to my wife Goska and my children Alexander and Julia — *Mark Jarrett*

TABLE OF CONTENTS

UNIT 1: LAYING A FOUNDATION

UNIT 2: ANSWERING DIFFERENT TYPES OF QUESTIONS

UNIT 3: REVIEW OF THE CONTENT STANDARDS

UNIT 4: A PRACTICE TEST

PHOTO CREDITS

Cover Photo: Situated alongside the Detroit River, the Renaissance Center is Detroit's most identifiable symbol. The Center's four cylindrical towers were completed in 1977 at a cost of $350 million. In 1996, General Motors Corporation bought the Renaissance Center for use as its company headquarters. © SuperStock, Inc.

CHAPTER 3 — DIFFERENT TYPES OF PROMPTS
Page 23: Library of Congress.

CHAPTER 6 — GEOGRAPHY
Page 42: United Nations. Page 44: United Nations; Page 45: © Stewart Milstein, Photographer; Page 47: Soviet Embassy; Page 50: United Nations (68430); Page 51: (t) Consulate General of the People's Republic of China, (b) United Nations.

CHAPTER 7 — HISTORY
Page 59: (t & m) Library of Congress, (b) NASA; Page 61: Library of Congress; Page 63: (t & b) Library of Congress; Page 64: New York State Archives; Page 65: Theodore Roosevelt Association; Page 67: Library of Congress; Page 68: Franklin D. Roosevelt Presidential Library; Page 69: (t) National Archives, (b) Library of Congress; Page 71: (t) Schomburg Center For Research in Black Culture, (b) National Archives; Page 73: (t) Library of Congress, (b) Bureau of Engraving and Printing; Page 74: (t) White House, (b) Ronald Reagan Presidential Library; Page 75: (t) Jarrett Archives, (b) White House; Page 80: Library of Congress.

CHAPTER 8 — ECONOMICS
Page 85: (t) United Nations, (m) U.S. Army, (b) © Stewart Milstein, Photographer; Page 86: United Nations; Page 87: United Nations; Page 88: Ford Motor Company; Page 89: Jarrett Archives; Page 90: Jarrett Archives; Page 91: National Archives; Page 92: Jarrett Archives; Page 94: Jarrett Archives; Page 95: (t) Bureau of Engraving and Printing, (b) © Stewart Milstein, Photographer; Page 100: Jarrett Archives; Page 101: Jarrett Archives; Page 102: Library of Congress.

CHAPTER 9 — CIVICS
Page 109 (t) John F. Kennedy Library, (m) © Stewart Milstein, Photographer, (b) Library of Congress; Page 112: U.S. Army; Page 117: (t) Library of Congress, (b) Schomberg Center for Research in Black Culture; Page 120: (t & b) Collection of the U.S. Supreme Court; Page 123: Smithsonian Institution, Freer Gallery of Art; Page 124: United Nations (176105) John Issac, Photographer; Page 126: National Archives; Page 127: (t) Jarrett Archives, (b) Amnesty International; Page 130: Collection of the U.S. Supreme Court.

CHAPTER 11 — PUBLIC DISCOURSE AND DECISION-MAKING
Page 143: (t,m,b) Jarrett Archives; Page 145: U.S. Capitol Society.

CHAPTER 12 — A PRACTICE HIGH SCHOOL TEST IN SOCIAL STUDIES
Page 170: Franklin D. Roosevelt Presidential Library.

CHAPTER 1

WHAT LIES AHEAD

Taking tests is something that all students must do. Everyone wants to do well on Michigan's **High School Test in Social Studies**. Unfortunately, just wanting to do well is not enough. You have to really work at it.

WHAT IS THE HIGH SCHOOL TEST IN SOCIAL STUDIES?

The purpose of social studies is to prepare young people to become responsible citizens. In 1996, the Michigan Board of Education approved a new set of content standards in social studies, along with a plan to measure each student's educational development. This plan called for a statewide test in social studies. Knowledge which meets these content standards will be very important for achieving a good grade on the test.

On the High School Test in Social Studies, you will be asked questions dealing with six categories called **strands**:

STRANDS
- ✦ geography
- ✦ history
- ✦ economics
- ✦ civics
- ✦ inquiry
- ✦ public discourse and decision-making

CONTENT STANDARDS

The strands cover 22 different **content standards**. Each content standard spells out part of what you are expected to know by the time you graduate from high school. The social studies content standards are listed on the following chart:

STRANDS

CONTENT STANDARDS

Social Studies Standards for the High School Test					
Historical Perspective	**Geographic Perspective**	**Civic Perspective**	**Economic Perspective**	**Inquiry**	**Public Discourse and Decision-Making**
I.1 Time and Chronology	**II.1** Peoples, Places and Cultures	**III.1** Purposes of Government	**IV.1** Individual and House-hold Choices	**V.1** Information Processing	**VI.1** Identifying and Analyzing Public Issues
I.2 Comprehend-ing the Past	**II.2** Human/ Environment Interaction	**III.2** Ideals of American Democracy	**IV.2** Business Choices		**VI.2** Persuasive Writing
I.3 Analyzing and Interpret-ing the Past	**II.3** Location, Movement and Connections	**III.3** Democracy in Action	**IV.3** Role of Government		
I.4 Judging Decisions from the Past	**II.4** Regions, Patterns and Processes	**III.4** American Government and Politics	**IV.4** Economic Systems		
	II.5 Global Issues and Events	**III.5** American Government and World Affairs	**IV.5** Trade		

THE BENCHMARKS

Each of the content standards contains one or more benchmarks. The benchmarks indicate what you should *specifically* know and be able to do at various grade levels. The benchmarks are used to trace your progress at different times during your educational career.

For example, let's look at the eleventh-grade benchmarks for the first content standard under the second strand, *Geographic Perspective*.

Strand: *Geographic Perspective*

Content Standard II.1:
Peoples, Places, and Cultures

All students will describe, compare, and explain the locations and characteristics of places, cultures, and settlements.

Benchmarks. By eleventh grade, students will:

- Describe how major world issues and events affect various people, societies, places, and cultures in different ways.

- Explain how culture might affect women's and men's perceptions.

As you can see, the *content standards* provide a general description of what students should be able to do. You will then be tested on your ability to do the specific things outlined in the *benchmarks* for your grade level. For example, the second benchmark *(shown above)* requires you to explain how culture affects women's and men's perceptions. This means you should be able to compare women's and men's perceptions in several different societies, such as the United States, Latin America, China, and the Middle East, and explain how these perceptions are influenced by culture.

To help you focus on what you must know and do for each benchmark, following each question in this book is the number of the benchmark being tested. In addition, at the end of each content chapter is a list of the benchmarks for the strand covered in that chapter.

THE TEST FORMAT

The questions on the High School Test in Social Studies all follow the same pattern. They ask you to apply the knowledge needed to meet the benchmark requirements. In particular, you must be able to apply this knowledge when analyzing a "prompt." A **prompt** is information presented in the question in the form of a reading, map, chart, graph, drawing, or other format. To understand the prompt, you must activate your *prior knowledge* — what you already know in social studies. Thus, to do well on this test, you have to:

   ✦ be able to meet the benchmark requirements, and

   ✦ be able to analyze information presented in different types of prompts.

HOW THIS BOOK IS ORGANIZED

For the High School Test, you will be responsible for what you have learned from the eighth grade through the middle of the eleventh grade. How can you be expected to re-member so much information? With this book as your guide, you should find the test easier, and maybe even fun to take. ***Mastering Michigan's High School Test in Social Studies*** will help you prepare to answer any type of question found on the test.

The following section-by-section review explains what you will find in this book.

UNIT 1: WHAT LIES AHEAD

This opening chapter, which you are now reading, describes how the book is organized and introduces you to the High School Test in Social Studies.

Chapter 2 gives you some powerful techniques for remembering information, which will be helpful in preparing for the High School Test and other tests as well.

UNIT 2: ANSWERING DIFFERENT TYPES OF QUESTIONS

This section of the book consists of three chapters. They focus on two of the three types of questions that appear on Michigan's High School Test. The third type of question, called an extended-response question, is covered in Chapter 11.

✦ **Chapter 3** deals with prompts. On the High School Test, each type of question begins with a prompt, which you must interpret.

✦ **Chapter 4** focuses on how to answer clusters of selected-response questions. In these questions, you will be asked to "select" the correct answer from a group of four possible choices.

✦ **Chapter 5** examines how to answer constructed-response questions. In these questions, you will be asked to perform a short task such as filling in a chart, creating a timeline, writing a paragraph, or completing a map.

UNIT 3: REVIEW OF THE CONTENT STRANDS

This section provides brief summaries of the information you need to review for each of the strands on Michigan's High School Test in Social Studies. Each chapter contains a capsule summary of the basic information you need to know for that strand. The summary is followed by a graphic organizer of the strand's major terms and concepts. Each chapter also has an explanation of the strand's benchmarks, and a series of practice questions. Each chapter concludes with a complete listing of that strand's benchmarks.

✦ **Chapter 6** reviews **geography**. It focuses on the geographic and environmental implications of global issues and events.

✦ **Chapter 7** reviews **history**. It summarizes the major eras of U.S. history from 1815 to the present.

✦ **Chapter 8** reviews **economics**. It emphasizes the major terms and concepts of economics. It also reviews the operation of the U.S. economy and its role in the world economy.

✦ **Chapter 9** reviews **civics**. It describes the American system of democratic government, including the structure of state and federal government in the United States. It also reviews America's role in world affairs.

✦ **Chapter 10** reviews **inquiry**. This chapter will show you how to answer constructed-response questions on the inquiry section of the test.

✦ **Chapter 11** reviews **public discourse and decision-making**, including the "core democratic values." The chapter shows you how to answer a sample extended-response question on a public policy issue, similar to the extended-response questions on the actual test.

UNIT 4: A PRACTICE TEST

The final section of this book contains a complete practice High School Test in Social Studies. You should take this practice test under conditions similar to those of the actual test. This practice test will help increase your confidence and allow you to spot areas of weakness that need further review. You can go over the answers with your teacher in class as a final review before taking the actual statewide test.

By paying careful attention to your teachers at school, by completing your homework assignments, and by preparing with this book, you can be confident that you will do your best when the day of the real High School Test arrives.

NOTE: To receive a Social Studies endorsement on your high school transcript, you need to pass the High School Test in Social Studies. The endorsement on your transcript may be a factor that some colleges take into consideration in their admissions policies.

CHAPTER 2

REMEMBERING IMPORTANT TERMS AND CONCEPTS

Have you ever watched workers building a house? You might have noticed that electricians, plumbers, bricklayers, and others use a variety of tools to help complete the job. Every good worker knows that the better the tools are, the better the work will be.

Like builders constructing a house, you need a good set of tools when you study. This chapter will supply you with some of these tools.

DEVELOPING VOCABULARY CARDS

Terms are words or phrases that refer to specific things. For example, *The Great Lakes* is a term. **Concepts** give a name to things that are not specific, such as general ideas or groups of things. *Democracy* is a concept. The High School Test in Social Studies will assess your knowledge of both terms and concepts.

Remember that the key to successful study is to take an active approach. One of the best ways to learn and remember a new term or concept is to create a vocabulary card. A **vocabulary card** is an index card on which you write important information about major terms and concepts.

To reinforce your learning, you should make vocabulary cards for the most important terms and concepts in each content area. The graphic organizers found in each content chapter of this book identify many of the terms and concepts you will need to know. Make a separate card for each one.

Each vocabulary card has two parts:

THE FRONT OF THE CARD

On the top line of the card, write the name of the term or concept. Below that line, define or explain it. Beneath the definition or explanation, provide an example, explain the importance of the term or concept, or give other important information about it. Use your textbook, school library, and the content summaries in this book to find the information you need to complete each card.

THE BACK OF THE CARD

On this side of the card, draw a picture that illustrates the term or concept. Your picture may show how something actually looks or may be symbolic. Turning the written information on the front of the card into an illustration on the back will help you to clarify the meaning of the term or concept. By illustrating the key points, you create a picture in your mind that will help you to remember the word or phrase.

Let's look at the term *Upper Peninsula*:

Front of card

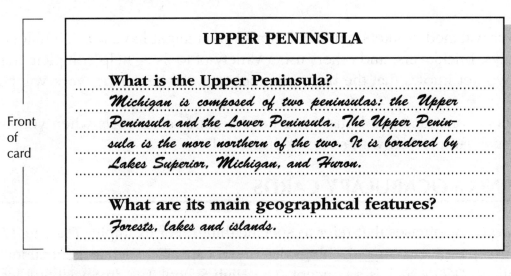

Back of card

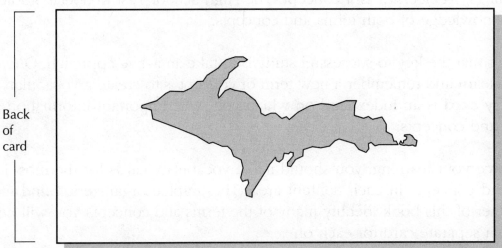

After you have completed a set of vocabulary cards, you can use them to help you prepare for the test.

✦ Look at the picture side of the card and try to recall the name of the term or concept.

✦ On the front of the card, look at the name of the term or concept. Try covering the rest of the card with your hand or a piece of paper. See how well you can recall the definition or example. Then remove your hand or the paper to see if you are correct.

USING MNEMONIC DEVICES

A very helpful tool for recalling factual information is a **mnemonic** (ne mon' ik) device. Mnemonic devices are word tricks that help you to remember information. They are especially useful when you have to memorize a list or group of items.

THE KEY WORD METHOD

To use this method, you take the *first letter* of each word on a list and arrange those letters to form a *new* word that is easy to remember. For example, a "key word" might be helpful for recalling the names of the five Great Lakes:

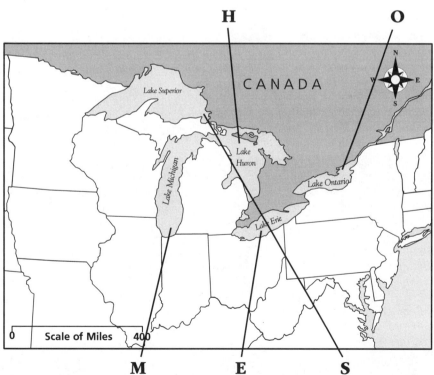

You can see that a handy key word for the names of the Great Lakes is **HOMES**. It uses the first letter in the name of each lake: **H**uron, **O**ntario, **M**ichigan, **E**rie, and **S**uperior.

10

THE KEY SENTENCE METHOD
Another mnemonic device is to create a "key sentence." For example, the flags of four
nations flew over parts of Michigan at different times: France, Spain, England, and the
United States. What would be an easy way to remember this group of nations?

1. Think of a word that rhymes with the name of each nation, or starts with the same
    letter or letters:

    ✦ United States — Uncle (both words start with "Un")
    ✦ France — Frank (both words start with "Fran")
    ✦ Spain — speaks (both words start with "sp")
    ✦ England — English (both words start with "Engl")

2. Now put these words together to form a sentence that will help you to remember
    the group of nations. For example:

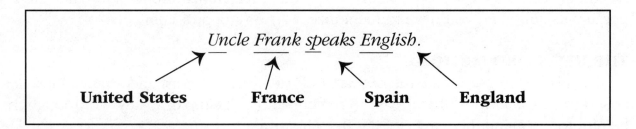

CHAPTER 3

DIFFERENT TYPES OF PROMPTS

On the High School Test in Social Studies, there will be three types of questions:

SELECTED-RESPONSE QUESTIONS   **CONSTRUCTED-RESPONSE QUESTIONS**   **EXTENDED-RESPONSE QUESTIONS**

Each of the questions assumes that you know how to interpret different types of prompts. You cannot begin to answer the questions unless you **understand the prompt.** In this chapter, you will examine the major types of prompts found on the test:

* Maps
* Bar Graphs
* Line Graphs
* Pie Charts

* Tables
* Timelines
* Drawings and Photographs
* Political Cartoons

* Reading Selections

Our discussion of each prompt will be divided into three parts:

1. A description of the type of prompt.

2. An examination of each part of the prompt to help you interpret it.

3. Comprehension questions to check your understanding. These questions will only test your ability to *interpret* prompts. They are not the same as model High School Test questions, which are found throughout the rest of this book.

MAPS

WHAT IS A MAP?

A map is a drawing that represents a geographic area. There are many kinds of maps. Some of the most common are:

♦ **Political maps**, showing the major boundaries between countries or states.

♦ **Physical maps**, showing the physical characteristics of a region, such as rivers, mountains, vegetation, and elevation *(height above sea level)*.

♦ **Theme maps**, providing information on a theme such as natural resources, rainfall, languages spoken, average temperatures, or main points of interest.

STEPS TO UNDERSTANDING A MAP

1. Look at the Title. The title of the map tells you what kind of information is presented. For example, the title of the map below shows that it concerns how land is used in the nation of Bangladesh.

2. Look at the Legend. The legend, also called the **key**, lists the symbols used and identifies what they represent. In this map:

◐ the medium gray areas show where land is used for forestry;

● the dark gray areas show where industry is located;

○ the light gray areas show where land is used for farming.

3. Look at the Compass Rose. It indicates the four basic directions: north, south, east, and west. Most maps show north at the top and south at the bottom. If no direction indicator appears, you can usually assume that north is at the top and south is at the bottom.

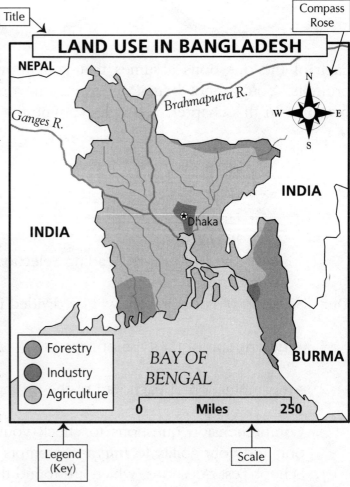

4. Look at the Scale. A map would be impossible to use if it were the same size as the area it shows. Mapmakers reduce the size so that it can fit onto a page. The scale indicates the actual distance between places on the map. The distance is usually shown in miles *(or kilometers)*. For example, on one map an inch may represent 1 mile, while on another map an inch may represent 100 miles.

Finding Specific Information. To find specific information, you must use the legend and other map features together. For example, if you wanted to find which areas of Bangladesh are the most industrialized, here is what you must do:

1. In the map legend on page 12, notice that *dark gray* indicates areas that have industry. Look for areas in dark gray on the map.

2. Small sections in both the central and southeastern parts of Bangladesh are shown in dark gray, indicating that these areas are where industries are located.

INTERPRETING A MAP
Now answer the following questions about the map on the previous page.

CHECKING YOUR UNDERSTANDING

What is most of the land in Bangladesh used for? _____

Name two major rivers that merge in Bangladesh before flowing into the Bay of

Bengal. _____

_____

BAR GRAPHS

WHAT IS A BAR GRAPH?
A bar graph is a chart made up of parallel bars of different lengths. A bar graph is often used to compare two or more things, and how they have changed over time.

Name_____ Teacher_____

STEPS TO UNDERSTANDING A BAR GRAPH

1. Look at the Title. The title tells you the topic of the graph. For example, the title of the following bar graph indicates that the graph shows where immigrants to the United States came from, between 1900 and 1995.

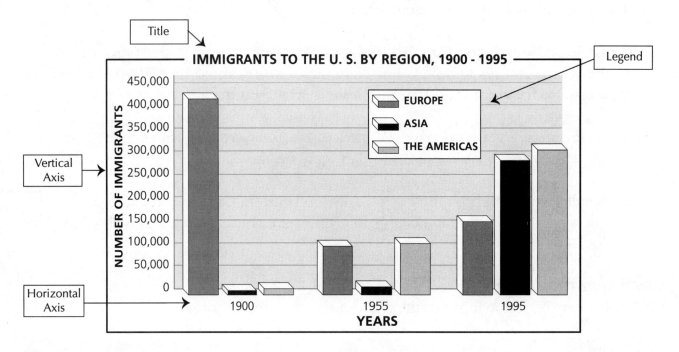

2. Look at the Legend. It shows what each bar represents. In the graph above:

- the dark gray bars represent Europe
- the black bars represent Asia
- the light gray bars represent the Americas *(North, Central, and South America)*

3. Look at the Vertical Axis and the Horizontal Axis.

- The **vertical axis** runs from top to bottom. It usually measures the length of the bars. Here, it lists the "Number of Immigrants" — from 0 to 450,000.

- The **horizontal axis** runs from left to right. It usually identifies the bars. Here the horizontal axis indicates the "Years" being compared: 1900, 1955, and 1995.

Note: Some bar graphs show bars running sideways. The only difference between an up-and-down bar graph and a sideways one is that the axes are reversed.

Finding Specific Information. To find specific information, you must examine the features of the bar graph closely. For example, to find out how many immigrants came to the United States from Europe in 1900, here is what to do:

1. On the horizontal axis, find the year 1900.

2. Choose the bar that represents Europe. According to the legend, this is the dark gray bar.

3. Run your finger to the top of the bar, and slide it slightly to the left. When you reach the vertical axis, you will find it is between 400,000 and 450,000. This shows that the number of immigrants from Europe in 1900 was about 425,000.

INTERPRETING A BAR GRAPH

Now that you have read about bar graphs, answer the following questions about the bar graph on the previous page.

CHECKING YOUR UNDERSTANDING

In which year — 1900, 1955, or 1995 — did the least number of Europeans come to the United States? _____

How many immigrants came to the United States from Asia in 1955? _____

LINE GRAPHS

What Is a Line Graph?

A line graph is a chart composed of a series of points connected by a line. A line graph is often used to show how something has changed over a period of time.

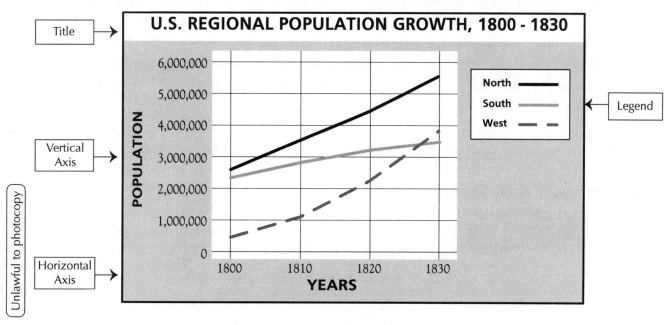

Name_____ Teacher_____

STEPS TO UNDERSTANDING A LINE GRAPH

1. Look at the Title. The title tells you the topic of the graph. In the graph on the previous page, the title indicates that this line graph compares regional population growth in the United States between 1800 and 1830.

2. Look at the Vertical Axis and the Horizontal Axis.

- The **vertical axis** runs from bottom to top. It often measures the size of something. As you move up the vertical axis, the numbers get larger. Note that the vertical axis in this line graph shows "Population."

- The **horizontal axis** runs from left to right. In this line graph, the horizontal axis shows "Years." The first year is 1800, and the dates continue in ten-year intervals until 1830.

3. Look at the Legend. If there is a legend, it explains what each line represents. If a line graph has only one or two lines, there is often no legend because the information is marked directly on the graph. In this graph, the legend tell us that:

- the **black** line indicates the **North's population**,
- the **gray** line indicates the **South's population**, and
- the **dashed** line indicates the **West's population**.

Finding Specific Information. For specific information, you must examine the two axes. For example, what was the North's population in 1820?

- First, run your finger across the horizontal axis until you reach the year 1820.

- Now move your finger up until you reach the line representing the North. To find the actual number, slide your finger to the left until you reach the numbers on the vertical axis. This point intersects about midway between the "4,000,000" and the "5,000,000" line.

- Thus, the North's population in 1820 was about 4,500,000 people.

INTERPRETING A LINE GRAPH

Now answer the following questions about the line graph on page 15.

CHECKING YOUR UNDERSTANDING

What was the difference in population between the South and West in 1800?

_____

In which section of the nation was population rising the fastest? _____

_____

PIE CHARTS

WHAT IS A PIE CHART?

A pie chart, also called a **circle graph**, is a circle divided into sections of different sizes. A pie chart is often used to show the relationship between a whole and its parts. When two pie charts are presented together, as in the example below, you can quickly compare relationships between years.

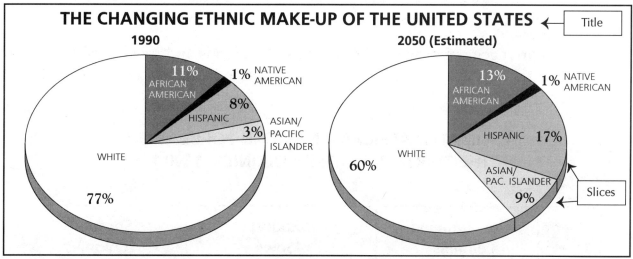

Source: *Statistical Abstract of the United States*

STEPS TO UNDERSTANDING A PIE CHART

1. Look at the Title. The title tells you the topic. For example, these pie charts show the ethnic make-up of the U.S. in 1990 and the estimated ethnic makeup in 2050.

2. Look at the Slices. Each slice shows its size or relationship to the whole pie. Think of the pie as 100% of something. If you add up all the slices, they total 100%. In each of these two pies, the five different ethnic groups that make up the U.S. population are named on the pie slices.

3. Look at the Legend. Sometimes a pie chart has a legend showing what each slice of the pie represents. If the information is shown on the slices, a legend is not needed.

Finding Specific Information

To find specific information, examine each slice. For example, to find out what percentage of the U.S. population was made up of African Americans in 1990, look for the slice marked "African Americans" on the pie chart for "1990." It was 11% of the total.

INTERPRETING A PIE CHART

Now answer the following questions about the pie charts on the previous page.

CHECKING YOUR UNDERSTANDING

Which group is expected to increase the most between 1990 and 2050?

_____

Which group is expected to be the same percentage in 2050 as in 1990?

_____

TABLES

What Is a Table?

A table is an arrangement of words or numbers in columns and rows. A table is often used to organize large amounts of information so that individual facts can be easily located and compared.

Title

ESTIMATED AFRICAN-AMERICAN POPULATION IN THE THIRTEEN BRITISH COLONIES, 1690-1750

Column Headings (Categories)

Rows

Year	New England Colonies	Middle Colonies	Southern Colonies
1690	905	2,472	13,307
1700	1,680	3,361	22,476
1710	2,585	6,218	36,063
1720	3,956	10,825	54,058
1730	6,118	11,683	73,220
1740	8,541	16,452	125,031
1750	10,982	20,736	204,702

Source: *Historical Statistics of the United States*

Name_____   Teacher_____

STEPS TO UNDERSTANDING A TABLE

1. Look at the Title. The title states the overall topic. For example, the table on the previous page provides information about the number of African Americans living in the thirteen British colonies of North America, from 1690 through 1750.

2. Look at the Categories. Each table has various categories of information. These categories are named in the **column headings** across the top of the table. In this table, there are four different categories: *Year, New England Colonies, Middle Colonies,* and *Southern Colonies.* The **rows** contain information for each category.

Finding Specific Information

For specific information, you must find where the **columns** and **rows** intersect. For example, if you want to know the total number of African Americans living in the Middle Colonies in 1730, here is what you must do:

- Put your right index finger on the column marked *Middle Colonies*. This column shows the African-American population in the Middle Colonies for various years.

- Put your left index finger on the column marked *Year*. Slide your finger down until it reaches the row for the year *"1730."*

- Slide your right finger down the *Middle Colonies* column to the *"1730"* row. You can see that the total number of African Americans living in the Middle Colonies in 1730 was 11,683.

INTERPRETING A TABLE

Now answer the following questions about the table on the previous page.

CHECKING YOUR UNDERSTANDING

What was the total number of African Americans living in the thirteen British colonies in 1740?

_____

Which section had the largest number of African Americans in 1750: the New England Colonies, the Middle Colonies, or the Southern Colonies?

_____

Name_____ Teacher_____

TIMELINES

WHAT IS A TIMELINE?

A timeline shows a group of events arranged in chronological order along a line. **Chronological order** is the order in which the events occurred. The *first* event to occur is the *first* event to appear on the timeline. The span of a timeline can be anything from a short period to several thousand years. The main function of a timeline is to show how events are related to each other. Timelines can be made horizontally or vertically, and you may see either kind on the High School Test in Social Studies.

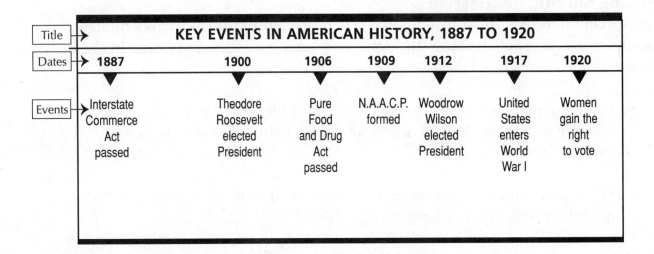

STEPS TO UNDERSTANDING A TIMELINE

1. Look at the Title. The title tells you the general topic. In the example above, the title indicates that the timeline lists important events or "milestones" in our country's history from 1887 through 1920.

2. Look at the Events. Events on the timeline are related to the title. For example, in this timeline each event was a major development of the Progressive Era.

3. Look at the Dates. Events are placed on the timeline in chronological order. A timeline is always based on a particular time period, no matter how brief or long. For example, this timeline starts in the later part of the 1800s and continues to 1920.

The space between events is usually proportional to the actual time that has passed. If you were to add another event, its date might fall between two existing dates on the timeline. For example, if you wanted to add the passage of the Federal Reserve Act in 1913 which reformed the banking industry, where would it go? Since 1913 is closer to 1912 *(1 year)* than it is to 1917 *(4 years)*, you would place it on the timeline closer to 1912 than to 1917.

4. Be Aware of Special Terms. To understand questions about timelines or time periods, you should be familiar with two special terms:

✦ A **decade** is a ten-year period.
✦ A **century** is a 100-year period.

> **Note:** Identifying centuries may seem confusing at first. For example, the 20th century refers to the 100 years from 1901 to 2000. This numbering system came about because we start counting from the year it is believed that Christ was born. Thus, the first one hundred years after the birth of Christ were the years 1-100. This time period is called the **first century**. The **second century** went from 101 to 200; the **third century** was from 201 to 300, and so on.

5. Look at the Passage of Time. Remember that events are arranged from the earliest event *(on the left)* to the most recent event *(on the right)*. To measure the number of years from one date to another, subtract the smaller date from the larger date. If it is the year 1999, how long has it been since Michigan was admitted as a state in 1837? By subtracting 1837 from 1999, we find that it was 162 years ago:

```
   1999  (assume this is the current year)
 - 1837  (the year Michigan was admitted as a state)
   162  years ago
```

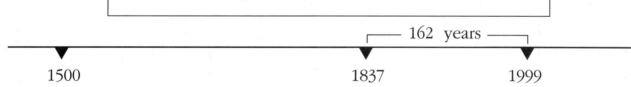

1500   1837   1999

162 years

INTERPRETING A TIMELINE

Now answer the following questions about the special terms related to timelines, and the timeline on page 20.

CHECKING YOUR UNDERSTANDING

Which century includes the years 1801-1900? _____

What will the next century, 2001-2100, be called? _____

On what time period does the timeline focus? _____

How many years are covered by the timeline? _____

Which event happened first: the passage of the Pure Food and Drug Act, or the start of World War I? _____

Name_____   Teacher_____

CREATING A TIMELINE

Let's put your understanding of timelines to work. Below is a list of events and when they occurred. Use this information to create a timeline.

> 1964: Lyndon Johnson elected President
> 1961: Bay of Pigs invasion fails
> 1960: John F. Kennedy elected President
> 1968: President Johnson declines to seek second term
> 1963: President Kennedy assassinated in Dallas
> 1962: John Glenn becomes first American to orbit Earth

Use the graphic below to create your timeline:

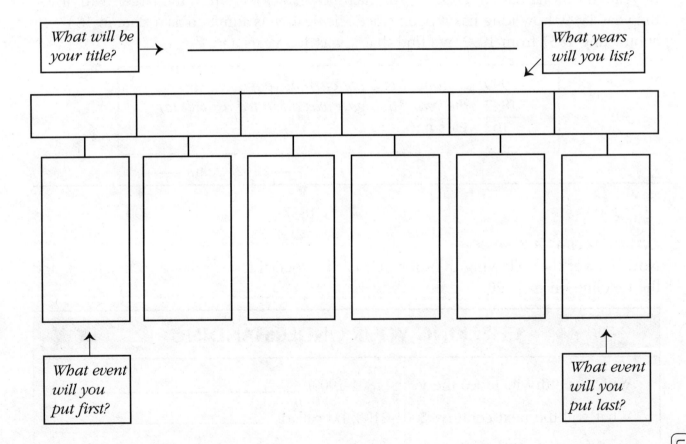

What will be your title?

What years will you list?

What event will you put first?

What event will you put last?

Name_____ Teacher_____

DRAWINGS AND PHOTOGRAPHS

WHAT IS A DRAWING OR PHOTOGRAPH?

A drawing or photograph shows how something looked in the past or looks today. Drawings and photographs are especially useful for understanding the past by showing how people looked and dressed, and what they once did.

Often, a photograph allows us to get the "feeling" of an earlier period of time or a different place. Since photography was not invented until the mid-1800s, we rely on artists' drawings and paintings to show what things looked like before that time.

Children after a day of work in a coal mine in 1870

STEPS TO UNDERSTANDING A DRAWING OR PHOTOGRAPH

1. Look at the Title or Caption. Most drawings or photographs have a title or caption that identifies what is being shown. For example, in the photograph above the caption is *Children after a day of work in a coal mine in 1870*.

2. Look at the Details. To find specific information, examine the *details* in the photograph or drawing. For example, if you want to know what child labor was like for some children in the 1870s, here is what to do:

- Look carefully at the physical details and consider what they might mean. For example, the boys in this picture are probably 10 to 12 years old. All of them are wearing hats, coveralls, and heavy gloves. Their faces are dirty. They don't look very healthy. Note also that none of the children are smiling — unusual for such a large group of boys.

- Based on this photograph, it seems clear that in the 1870s one group of people who worked in coal mines were young boys. Eventually, laws were passed in the early 1900s that prevented the use of child labor in the United States.

INTERPRETING A DRAWING OR PHOTOGRAPH

Now that you have looked at the details, answer the following questions based on the photograph on the previous page.

CHECKING YOUR UNDERSTANDING

Do you think these boys enjoyed their work? _____

Explain. _____

_____

Do you think these children attended school? _____

Explain. _____

_____

What kind of work do you think these boys did in the mine? _____

_____

_____

Name_____   Teacher_____

POLITICAL CARTOONS

WHAT IS A POLITICAL CARTOON?
A political cartoon is a drawing that expresses an opinion about a topic or issue. Many political cartoons are humorous, but the point they make is usually serious.

KEYS TO UNDERSTANDING A POLITICAL CARTOON

1. Look at the Title or Caption. Many political cartoons will have a title or caption. The title or caption will give insight or meaning to the message the cartoonist is trying to get across.

2. Look at Objects Used to Persuade. Cartoonists want to persuade readers to follow their point of view. They will use the size of objects, facial expressions, exaggerations or spoken words to make fun of some positions and to support others. Sometimes a cartoonist simply wants to draw attention to a particular issue. Cartoonists also show famous individuals closely associated with a particular issue or country. A *caricature* is a drawing in which a subject's features are deliberately exaggerated to produce a comic effect.

3. Be Aware of Symbols. Cartoonists often use **symbols** — objects that stand for, or represent, something else. Animals are often used as symbols. For example, an elephant sometimes represents the Republican Party, while a donkey is used as a symbol of the Democratic Party:

| THE REPUBLICAN PARTY | THE DEMOCRATIC PARTY |

INTERPRETING A POLITICAL CARTOON
In order to understand the meaning of a cartoon, it helps to know something about the background of the situation it depicts. What do you know about the background to the situation depicted in the cartoon on the next page?

Adrift in Dangerous Waters?

FINDING SPECIFIC INFORMATION

To find specific information, you must examine the cartoon carefully. For example, if you want to understand this cartoon, here is what you must look at:

- The cartoonist has drawn a boat labeled the U.S.S. America. The boat is a symbol representing contemporary American society. The boat is surrounded by sharks, symbolizing some of the problems that threaten us, such as pollution, crime, and poverty. There is a danger that the sharks might kill the people in the boat.

- The caption, "Adrift in dangerous waters?" implies that the American people are drifting in unsafe waters without a clear direction and may be in danger of being overwhelmed by these problems.

INTERPRETING A POLITICAL CARTOON

Now answer the following questions about the cartoon above.

CHECKING YOUR UNDERSTANDING

Which items in the cartoon are exaggerated or highlighted? _____

_____

Name one other problem the cartoonist might have included: _____

_____

Name_____ Teacher_____

READING SELECTIONS

WHAT IS A READING SELECTION?

A reading selection consists of a statement or group of statements about a particular topic or subject. It may be one or more brief quotations or short paragraphs. The main function of a reading selection is to present information or ideas about a topic.

STEPS TO UNDERSTANDING A READING SELECTION

To better understand a reading selection you should note that the writer presents a series of facts to support a point of view. Ask yourself the following questions about each reading selection:

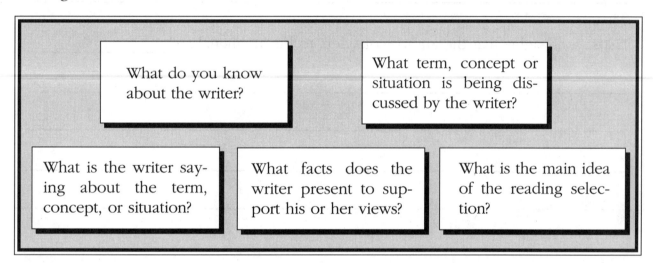

What do you know about the writer?

What term, concept or situation is being discussed by the writer?

What is the writer saying about the term, concept, or situation?

What facts does the writer present to support his or her views?

What is the main idea of the reading selection?

[A]ll men are created equal ... they are endowed by their Creator with certain unalienable Rights, [and] among these are Life, Liberty and the pursuit of Happiness. [T]o secure these rights, Governments are instituted among Men, deriving their just powers from the consent of the governed ... whenever any Form of Government becomes destructive of these ends, it is the right of the People to alter or abolish it, and to institute new Government ...

—Thomas Jefferson, *The Declaration of Independence, 1776*

INTERPRETING A READING SELECTION
Now answer the following questions about the reading selection on page 27.

CHECKING YOUR UNDERSTANDING

What is the main idea of the selection? _____

_____

_____

List several rights that the author considers to be "unalienable:" _____

_____

_____

_____

Name_____ Teacher_____

CHAPTER 4

ANSWERING CLUSTERS OF SELECTED-RESPONSE QUESTIONS

There will be three types of questions on Michigan's High School Test in Social Studies: selected-response, constructed and extended-response questions. This chapter explains how to answer clusters of **selected-response** questions.

THE STRUCTURE OF THE QUESTION

Selected-response clusters consist of a prompt followed by five multiple-choice questions. You will first be asked to read and study the prompt. Then for each question, you will need to select the best answer from among four possible choices.

WHAT IS BEING TESTED?

In selected-response clusters, you are being tested on **two** things:

✦ **Understanding the Prompt.** The prompt on which these questions are based will vary. It could be a short reading, a map, a chart, a graph, a drawing, a photograph, or a combination of these. In this chapter we assume that you know how to read and interpret the prompt. Chapter 3 has already focused on interpreting prompts.

✦ **Understanding the Benchmarks.** You will also need to use your prior social studies knowledge to choose the correct answer. This prior knowledge will be based on your mastery of the **benchmarks** of Michigan's curriculum for social studies.

> **REMEMBER:** You will **NOT** be able to answer the questions just from your understanding of the prompt. You will have to use both the **prompt** and your **knowledge based on the social studies benchmarks**.

A SAMPLE SELECTED-RESPONSE CLUSTER

Let's take a look at a typical selected-response cluster that might appear on the High School Test in Social Studies. The following cluster tests your ability to interpret a reading passage and your prior knowledge of the principles of American government.

Directions: Read the following passage and use it with what you already know to answer the questions that follow.

BROWN v. BOARD OF EDUCATION (1954)

In 1953, Linda Brown, an African-American student in Topeka, Kansas, was denied admission to an all-white public school near her home. The N.A.A.C.P. alleged that segregated public schools denied African-American children the "equal protection" of the laws guaranteed in the U.S. Constitution. They appealed a lower court ruling to the U.S. Supreme Court. In its decision, a unanimous Court wrote the following:

Does segregation of children in public schools solely on the basis of race, even though the physical facilities and other "tangible" factors may be equal, deprive the children of the minority group of equal educational opportunities? We believe it does. To separate them from others ... solely because of their race generates a feeling of inferiority as to their status in the community that may affect their hearts and minds in a way unlikely ever to be undone ... We conclude that in the field of public education, "separate-but-equal" has no place. Separate educational facilities are inherently unequal.

---

1 What role of the U.S. Supreme Court does this case illustrate?

   A Determining the constitutionality of federal laws
   B Enacting state laws
   C Interpreting our nation's constitution
   D Defining the standards for protecting accused persons

   III.1.HS.2

2 Which idea is reflected by the fact that in this case the U.S. Supreme Court was able to overturn a state law?

   A The U.S. government has a system of checks and balances.
   B The President of the United States is more powerful than any state governor.
   C The U.S. Constitution is the supreme law of the land.
   D State governments reserve certain powers to themselves.

   III.1.HS.2

Name _____ Teacher _____

3 If you were a lawyer representing the N.A.A.C.P. in this case, which of the following could BEST be used to support your argument?

    A Articles of Confederation   **C** Emancipation Proclamation

    B Bill of Rights   **D** Fourteenth Amendment

> III.2.HS.1

4 What was the importance of the decision in this case?

    A It caused the President to introduce Affirmative Action programs.

    B It increased state powers over educational matters.

    C It prohibited racial segregation in public schools.

    D It gave control of education to the federal government.

> III.3.HS.1

5 If you had been asked to speak at Linda Brown's trial, which core democratic value would you have used to support her position?

    A Federalism   **C** Separation of powers

    B Equal protection of the laws   **D** Popular sovereignty

> III.2.HS.1

EXPLANATION OF ANSWERS

1 What role of the U.S. Supreme Court does this case illustrate?

> The answer is **C**. You should realize the U.S. Supreme Court is the highest court in the nation. The role of the U.S. Supreme Court is to interpret the U.S. Constitution, both for the federal government and the states. An individual can appeal either a state or federal court decision to the U.S. Supreme Court if the case involves interpreting our nation's constitution. This question tests your understanding of how our federal system works. The benchmark tested here is III.1.HS.2.*

2 Which idea is reflected by the fact that in this case the U.S. Supreme Court was able to overturn a state law?

> The answer is **C**. Under our federal system, conflicts sometimes arise as to whether a state or federal law is permissible under the U.S. Constitution. The U.S. Constitution is our highest law. Like the previous question, this tests your understanding of our federal system. The benchmark tested here is III.1HS.2.

* The benchmarks for each strand are listed at the end of each chapter review for that strand.

Name _____ Teacher _____

3 If you were a lawyer representing the N.A.A.C.P. in this case, which of the following could BEST be used to support your argument?

> The answer is **D**. The U.S. Constitution and its amendments form the basis of our legal system. The Fourteenth Amendment guarantees all citizens the "equal protection" of the laws. Equal protection is specifically mentioned in the reading passage. The Fourteenth Amendment has been crucial to achieving equality for diverse groups. The benchmark tested here is III.2.HS.1.

4 What was the importance of the decision in this case?

> The answer is **C**. You should realize that in this case, the U.S. Supreme Court prohibited racial segregation in public schools. The question tests your ability to use actual cases to evaluate the effectiveness of our courts in the United States. The benchmark tested here is III.3.HS.1.

5 If you had been asked to speak at Linda Brown's trial, which core democratic value would you have used to support her position?

> The answer is **B**. One of the most important core democratic values is each person's right to equal protection of the laws. The Fourteenth Amendment forbids state governments to "... deny to any person within its jurisdiction the equal protection of the laws." As the reading notes, Brown's lawyers argued that she was denied "equal protection" by being required to attend a "black" school. The question tests your ability to identify the benefits and challenges of diversity in American life. The benchmark tested here is III.2.HS.1.

CHAPTER 5

ANSWERING CONSTRUCTED-RESPONSE QUESTIONS

Unlike selected-response questions, in which you *select* an answer from four choices, **constructed-response questions** require you to *create* your own answer. Like selected-response questions, this type of question tests your understanding of the benchmarks. There will be five constructed-response questions on the High School Test in Social Studies — one for each strand: geography, history, economics, civics, and inquiry.

THE "ACTION WORDS"

Constructed-response questions ask you to write something. They may ask you to identify and explain the consequences of something, to identify reasons to support or reject something, or to classify the positive or negative effects of something. What each question requires you to write about will be stated in the "**action words**" of the question. Following are some of the most common action words and hints on how to respond to them.

✦ **IDENTIFY**

Identify means to **name** or give the distinguishing characteristics of something. It is generally used when you name one or more places, people, or things.

- **Sample Question:** *Identify* two U.S. Presidents during the Progressive Era.

- **Hint:** To identify something is to name it or give its distinguishing features. You do not have to explain it further.

- **Model Answer:**

> *Two presidents of the United States during the Progressive Era were Theodore Roosevelt and Woodrow Wilson.*

✦ **DESCRIBE**

Describe means to **tell about** something — to present its special characteristics.

- **Sample Question**: *Describe* the European Union.

- **Hints**: To describe something is usually to tell about the *what, who, when,* and *where*. Start by answering the *what* first. Try to draw a word picture of *what* you are describing. Then answer the *who, when,* and *where* if they apply.

- **Model Answer**:

> *The European Union is an organization of European states that have established a unified economic market. Once known as the European Community or Common Market, the European Union has abolished all tariffs against members and allows a free flow of goods and services among members. In 1991, the Common Market decided to rename itself the European Union and to adopt a single currency and central bank.*

> **A Note About "Analyze":** Some questions on the High School Test in Social Studies may ask you to "analyze." To *analyze* something, you must break apart its elements and describe each one. Thus, when asked to analyze, it is advisable to follow the same steps as you would for *describe*.

Often on the High School Test you will be asked both to identify and describe something. Answer this type of question in two steps: first *identify*, and then *describe*.

- **Sample Question**: *Identify* a major era in American history and *describe* its defining characteristics.

- **Model Answer**:

Identifies   Describes

> *The industrialization of America in the late nineteenth century was an important era in U.S. history. During this period, railroads were built connecting cities, the countryside, and natural resources. Factories began to mass-produce goods. People moved into cities in large numbers, and immigrants poured into the United States.*

✦ **EXPLAIN AND SHOW**
Explain and **show** are often linked to the additional word *how* or *why*. Sometimes these instructions are even used interchangeably. The key in approaching any question with these particular "action words" is to determine whether it asks you to give an answer for *how* something happened or *why* it happened.

HOW QUESTIONS
In this type of question, the words "explain how" or "show how" are followed by a general statement that asks you to explain "how" something comes about or "how"

it relates to something else. You may be asked to show *how* the parts of a process or thing work together to bring about some effect.

- **Sample Question**: *Explain how* culture might affect women's perceptions.

- **Hints**: You must give factual examples that explain *how* women's perceptions are shaped by the culture in which they live.

- **Model Answer**:

> *Culture often affects women's perceptions, especially about their own role in society. For example, in traditional China women had to follow the will of the head of the family, who was the eldest male. They had no choice as to whom they married, where they lived or what work they did. In that culture, most women accepted this inferior role. In China today, cultural values have been affected by Westernization and Communism. Women have an equal role in the work force and perceive themselves as the equals of men.*

WHY QUESTIONS

Explain why or *show why* questions generally focus on causes. To *explain why* means to give one or more reasons why an event took place or to *show why* a relationship identified in the question occurred.

- **Sample Question**: Explain why Northern and Southern states went to war in 1861.

- **Hints**: You must present reasons or causes that explain *why* the event occurred. Here you need to explain *why* the North and South went to war.

- **Model Answer**:

> *Northern and Southern states went to war in 1861 for a number of reasons. The North and South had different economies and ways of life. The South was dependent on exporting cotton grown by slaves. Northern abolitionists, convinced that slavery was immoral, were determined to end it. The crisis became acute when the U.S. expanded westward. Each time new states were added to the Union, there was a struggle over whether they should permit slavery. The Republican candidate, Abraham Lincoln, was elected in 1860. The Southern states feared he would abolish slavery, and they seceded from the Union. To preserve the Union, Lincoln went to war with the Southern states.*

Now that you have studied the "action words," review the sample constructed-response question on the following pages.

A SAMPLE QUESTION

Directions: You should take about 5 minutes to read the following and use it with what you already know to complete this task.

Each year *Time* magazine selects its "Person of the Year." The selection by the magazine focuses on a person the editors believe has had a global impact. The following lists some of the people who have been chosen by *Time*:

Person of the Year

1938: **Adolf Hitler**
1939: **Joseph Stalin**
1952: **Queen Elizabeth II**
1963: **Martin Luther King, Jr.**
1977: **Anwar Sadat**
1979: **Ayatollah Khomeini**
1984: **Pope John Paul II**
1985: **Deng Xiaoping**
1986: **Corazon Aquino**
1987: **Mikhail Gorbachev**

On the lines provided, select *one* individual from the list. Describe one change that individual helped bring about, and the global consequences of that change.

Description of a change brought about by that individual and its global consequences:

_____

_____

_____

_____

_____

_____

_____

_____

_____

_____

_____

_____

_____

_____

The benchmark tested in this question asks you to "select individuals from the past that have had global impact on the modern world and describe their impact." [I.2.HS.2]

A MODEL ANSWER

The following represents a model answer.

Description of a change brought about that individual and its global consequences:

Mikhail Gorbachev became the leader of the Communist Party of the Soviet Union in 1984. He came to power in the Soviet Union at a time when his country was falling behind the West and was facing growing political and economic problems. Gorbachev introduced greater openness to Soviet society and started important economic reforms. Under Gorbachev, the Iron Curtain was lifted from Eastern Europe and democratic governments were elected there. As a result of Mikhail Gorbachev's courage and moral strength, the Cold War with the United States came to an end, and millions of people around the world were given new freedom and new opportunities.

Here you identify the person selected

Here you describe a change that the person brought about

Here you describe the global consequences of that change

CHAPTER 6

GEOGRAPHY

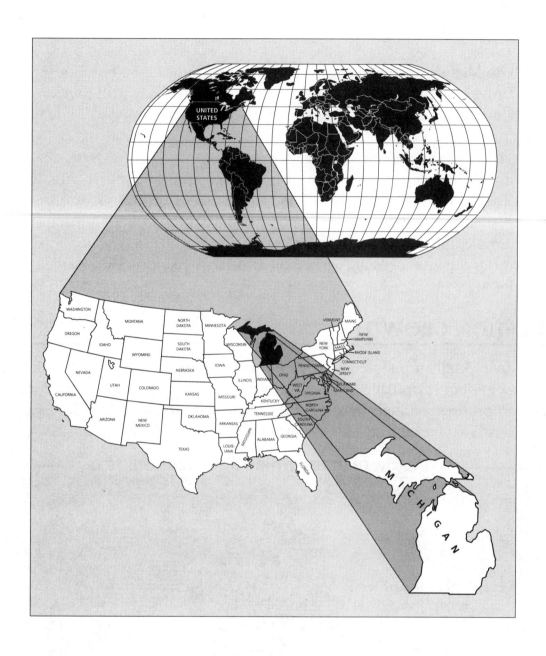

SECTION 1

A CAPSULE SUMMARY OF GEOGRAPHY

To do well on Michigan's High School Test in Social Studies, you must know about major world issues and processes and how they affect different world regions. You must also know how geography influences major world events.

The world today is changing at a rate never experienced before. Such changes make countries more **interdependent** than at any other time in history. This interdependence has helped to "shrink" the world and turn it into a **global village**. As the world has grown "smaller," problems in any one area have an increased impact on other areas. For example, the effects of pollution and environmental destruction are not limited by national borders. As a result, we are all affected by some of the same global processes and issues.

POPULATION GROWTH

There are over 5 billion people in the world today. This number doubles almost every 60 years. Continuing population growth threatens to overrun the ability of developing countries to produce enough housing, fuel, and food. To slow or reduce population, many nations have introduced birth control measures and family planning counseling.

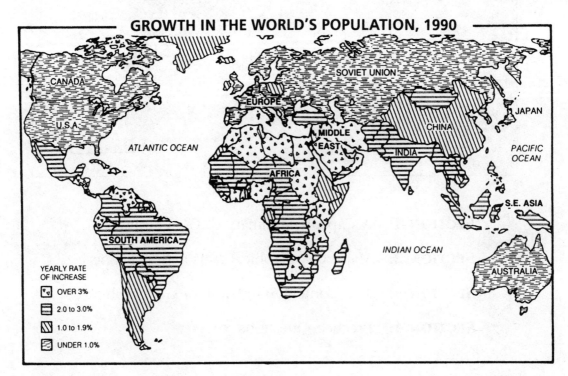

GROWTH IN THE WORLD'S POPULATION, 1990

Impact on Regions. **Developed nations**, such as the United States and the countries of Western Europe, have modest population growth. However, rapid population growth continues to be a serious problem for **developing nations** — countries in the Middle East, South and Southeast Asia, Latin America, and Africa. In the world's two largest nations, China and India, population growth poses a special challenge.

- **China**. There are over 1 billion people in China, nearly one out of every five people in the world. To slow down population growth, Chinese leaders have developed the "one-child" policy, which rewards families that have only one child.

- **India**. India is the world's second most populous nation. As a result of improved health care, limited knowledge of modern birth control, and the fact that parents traditionally have many children, India's population growth rate is very high. Indian leaders have tried to encourage greater use of birth control.

ECONOMIC DEVELOPMENT

The need for economic development remains the greatest challenge for developing nations. Most of these countries were colonized by European nations in the 19th and early 20th centuries. The vast majority of the local population worked as unskilled laborers or at subsistence farming. Meanwhile, the colonial elite imported manufactured goods from Europe. Even the nations of Latin America, which gained their independence at the beginning of the 19th century, remained dependent on exporting raw materials and cash crops to Europe and developed very little local manufacturing.

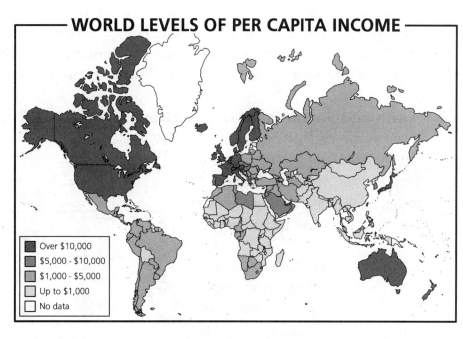

WORLD LEVELS OF PER CAPITA INCOME

- ■ Over $10,000
- ▨ $5,000 - $10,000
- ▤ $1,000 - $5,000
- ▢ Up to $1,000
- □ No data

After World War II, the countries of the colonial world achieved independence. In less than 20 years, India, Africa, the Middle East, and Southeast Asia threw off foreign rulers and established sovereign nations. The greatest task these new nations faced was to develop their own economies. They needed to establish new industries, increase agricultural output, educate their citizens, and develop a skilled workforce. They also had to build and improve hospitals, roads, housing, electricity, and communications.

42

To achieve these goals, developing countries often had to overcome natural obstacles such as harsh climates, a lack of key natural resources, or infertile soil. They also had to compete with more developed nations in world markets. Whatever economic gains these countries made were often swept aside by increased population growth, natural disasters, corruption, or civil war.

Traditional farming methods are still used in many developing countries.

Impact on Regions. To cope with the problems of economic development, the nations of the developing world adopted a variety of strategies.

- **Communist Nations**. In Communist nations like China, Vietnam, Cuba, and the former Soviet Union, the government controlled all the means of production. Five-year plans dictated how the nation's resources and energies would be spent, and frequently favored heavy industry and a powerful military. Such government ownership and control were often attractive to the leaders of struggling nations, but were not usually as successful as expected in fostering growth.

- **Africa**. The standards of living and incomes in Africa remain among the lowest in the world. After achieving independence, leaders in Africa often established dictatorships that controlled the economy. They attempted to develop local industries to avoid reliance on imports, but frequently ignored agriculture. Poor planning and political instability sometimes led to disastrous effects on the economy.

- **South and Southeast Asia**. The **Green Revolution** applied modern technology, such as the use of fertilizers and new crop breeds, to farming. This has allowed the farmers of India, Southeast Asia, and other countries to grow more food.

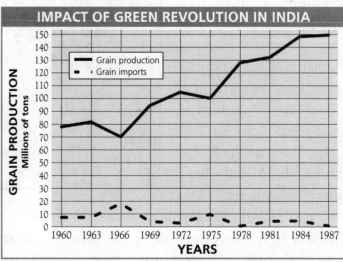

- **Latin America**. Latin American countries benefited from active trade with the United States and Europe. Latin American elites frequently invested overseas rather than in their own economies. In the late 1970s, many countries in Latin America borrowed from American and European banks to finance internal improvements, greatly increasing their international debt. In the

1980s, several of these countries had difficulty in making payments on these loans, creating concern among foreign lenders such as American banks. To end this crisis, foreign banks agreed to reduce the size of the debts these countries owed. At the same time, Latin American nations continue to suffer from the wide income gap separating the rich and poor.

- **Middle East**. In the 1960s, countries like Egypt experimented with **Arab Socialism**, which led to state ownership of some industries. Developing nations with oil formed an organization known as **OPEC** and sharply increased their prices in the 1970s. In this way, several Middle East countries, such as Saudi Arabia and Kuwait, were able to transform themselves into some of the world's richest nations.

In the 1970s, developing nations called upon the developed nations to pay reparations to former colonial areas in the form of massive economic aid. This demand met with little success, although it encouraged the OPEC countries to increase their prices.

In the 1980s, many developing nations found that the most promising path to development was to encourage foreign investment and a free market economy. The **World Bank** and **International Monetary Fund** helped by providing loans and economic aid. Many countries in Asia, including China, achieved remarkable growth rates by adopting this approach. However, in the late 1990s, some of the Southeast Asian economies faced a new economic crisis when their currencies collapsed.

URBANIZATION

Urbanization refers to the movement of people into cities. Poverty, as well as the need for fewer farmers due to modernization, have driven millions of people in developing nations (also known as the *Third World*) to emigrate to cities in search of jobs and education. Rising urban populations often require more food, water, electricity, schools, and medicines than cities can provide. Overcrowding leads to air pollution, traffic jams, and mounting garbage and sewage problems. Rural newcomers also face the challenge of confronting new values, often leading to great cultural stress. As people move to

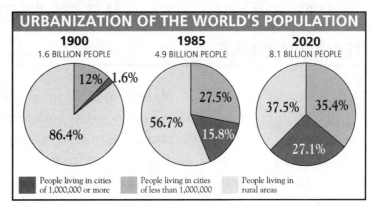

cities in ever-increasing numbers, they often lose touch with their past, their village, and family. These individuals undergo a crisis of identity, as they struggle between old and new values and suffer from feelings of isolation. Economic difficulties and the gap between the poor and the rich make this isolation all the more painful.

Impact on Regions. Urbanization often has a dramatic effect on developing nations.

- **Latin America**. In Latin America, people are migrating from the countryside to the cities in search of work, education, and better living. Many migrants settle in shanty towns on the outskirts of cities. The sheer size of these cities poses problems, since rapid urban growth often outstrips available public services and facilities.

- **Africa.** Most of Africa's people still live in villages in the countryside, but in only a few decades the majority will probably be living in cities. This rapid urbanization threatens to outstrip employment prospects and existing public services. Rapid urban growth has already led to the growth of shanty towns on the outskirts of many African cities, where people are crowded together in unsanitary conditions.

The modern city of Kinshasa, in Zaire

- **Middle East**. In the Middle East, people traditionally lived in villages where they farmed or herded livestock. The eldest male made family decisions, and marriages were arranged. Since the 1960s, large numbers have migrated to cities where they have suddenly made contact with a local middle class with Western values. Women's roles were expanded, traditions were questioned, and family influence weakened. These sudden changes have caused some groups in the Middle East to attack Westernization and to call for a return to traditional values through **Islamic Fundamentalism**.

- **South and East Asia**. Most people still live in villages, but large numbers have migrated into some of the world's largest and most crowded cities.

RESOURCE USE

Natural resources include plants, animals, and minerals. They are used to grow food, supply energy, make clothes and houses, and as raw materials for industry. Because of the uneven distribution of world resources, some nations attempt to acquire resources they lack through conquest or trade. Since most resources are in limited supply, it is important to conserve and recycle them.

Impact on Regions. Countries in North Africa and the Middle East with large oil reserves have profited by membership in OPEC, which attempts to limit production and control oil prices. Although they have oil, these countries lack fresh water for agriculture and human use. They must therefore trade their oil for food and other goods. High oil prices also can lead to competition for oil reserves, and in fact contributed to Iraq's long war with Iran and later invasion of neighboring Kuwait.

Japan provides an example of a country that lacks many important natural resources. In the early 20th century, Japan began a campaign of conquest to obtain those resources, but lost its conquered territories at the end of World War II. Today, Japan concentrates on using its skilled workforce and advanced technology to produce goods it can sell to other countries, to pay for the oil and other resources Japan must import.

INTERNATIONAL TRADE

In our interdependent global economy, all nations are affected by international trade. The availability of foreign goods encourages each nation to focus on producing those things it does best. While tariffs can restrict international trade, a large number of nations have entered into trading blocs, like NAFTA and the European Union.

Impact on Regions. Countries have cooperated globally to reduce trade barriers by negotiating the **General Agreement on Tariffs and Trade** (GATT) and establishing a World Trade Organization (WTO). At

Ocean-going freighters carry goods world-wide

the same time, many regions of the world promote trade with their neighbors by establishing regional associations.

- **Europe**. The European Economic Community was begun by several Western European nations to exchange goods and services without charging tariffs. In 1991, these countries decided to transform their association into a **European Union**. Eventually, they will merge their national currencies and create a European central bank.

- **North America**. Another regional trade association was created by the United States, Canada, and Mexico when they signed **NAFTA** — the North American Free Trade Agreement. The three nations have agreed to eventually eliminate all tariffs on goods from one another.

ENVIRONMENTAL IMPACT

Population growth, industrialization, and urbanization now pose a serious threat to the world's natural environment. Air pollution has led to the destruction of part of the ozone layer which protects the Earth from the harmful effects of solar radiation.

Carbon dioxide emissions and other pollutants have led to a world-wide warming known as the "**greenhouse effect**." Pol-lution threatens our rivers, lakes, oceans, and soil. The clearing of forests, especially tropical rain forests, reduces the world's supply of oxygen and threatens the exist-ence of many unique plant and animal species. World climate changes have led to desertification in some regions, threat-ening the lives of millions of people.

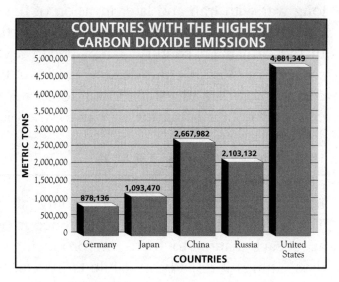

COUNTRIES WITH THE HIGHEST CARBON DIOXIDE EMISSIONS

Impact on Regions. Environmental de-struction and pollution do not recognize national borders and threaten all regions.

- **The Western Hemisphere.** The forests of North America are being damaged by **acid rain**, formed when sulfur is emitted by industrial activity. The Amazon rain forest is threatened by the Brazilian government's program to cut down and sell hardwood trees, clearing the land for farming. When rain forests are cut down, heavy rains wash away the soil. The destruction of rain forests also threatens the survival of unique plants and animals and reduces the world's oxygen supply.

- **Eastern Europe and Russia.** Under Communism, heavy industries were devel-oped without regard for the environment. This region is extremely polluted, in-cluding radioactivity from a nuclear power plant accident at **Chernobyl**, Ukraine.

- **Africa.** Global warming threatens the **Sahel** region — south of the Sahara — with **desertification** (*turning the land into a desert*), because of repeated droughts. Overgrazing has made the situation worse, and millions now face starvation.

At an international environmental conference in Rio de Janeiro, Brazil in 1992, nations pledged to reduce pollution and stop the destruction of the ozone layer and rain forests.

POLITICAL CHANGE

One of the most important processes affecting our world is political change. The 1980s and 1990s have witnessed a flowering of democratic governments. One important rea-son for this has been the collapse of Communism, which has encouraged supporters of democracy everywhere.

Impact on Regions. The Soviet Union became the world's first Communist society af-ter World War I. After World War II, Communism spread to Eastern Europe, China, Cuba, and other countries. However, by the 1980s Soviet Communism was in crisis.

Attempts to introduce reforms ignited nationalist feelings, leading to the dissolution of the Soviet Union. The breakup of the Soviet Union, the downfall of Communism, the end of the Cold War, and the lifting of the "Iron Curtain" from Eastern Europe have set in motion a series of global effects.

Statues of Lenin were toppled in former Communist countries

- **Eastern Europe and the former Soviet Union.** Former Communist countries in Eastern Europe and some of the republics of the former Soviet Union now have democratic governments. However, many of their citizens are not familiar with democracy or the workings of a free market economy. They find it hard to cope with the challenges of capitalism and self-rule.

- **China.** Although China still has a Communist political system, it has opened itself to foreign investment and adopted most features of a free market economy.

- **Germany.** In 1989, the East German Communist government resigned. The new democratic government lifted all travel restrictions, knocked down the **Berlin Wall** — the symbol of the Cold War — and reunited with West Germany.

- **Southeast Asia.** In the Philippines, dictator Ferdinand Marcos agreed to new elections and stepped down in favor of a popularly elected President.

- **Latin America.** Dictators and military governments in Haiti, Chile, Argentina, and other countries were replaced by newly-elected democratic governments. In Nicaragua, the Communist Sandinistas peacefully handed power over to an opposition political party after elections were held.

- **Africa.** Dictators have been driven out of countries such as Uganda, Ethiopia, and Mozambique. Several nations have switched from single-party to multi-party states.

ETHNIC UNREST

An **ethnic group** consists of a group of people united by cultural bonds. These bonds can come from a common language, race, history, or religion. African and Native American tribes, Eastern European nationalities, and South Asian religious groups (*Hindus, Sikhs, and Muslims*) are all examples of such ethnic groups.

Impact on Regions. All around the world, ethnic differences remain important sources of social and political conflict.

- **Middle East.** Israel was created in 1948 as a Jewish state surrounded by Arab nations. Differences between Israeli Jews and Palestinian Arabs have fueled more than forty years of violence throughout the region.

- **Africa. Tribalism** — allegiance to one's tribe — has created problems for African leaders who want their citizens to be loyal to the nation. European powers had created colonies in Africa without regard for ancient tribal boundaries. With independence, rival tribes often found themselves within the same country. This has led to conflicts. For example, animosity between Hutus and Tutsis in Rwanda led to the massacre of hundreds of thousands of people, mostly members of the Tutsi tribe, in 1996. **Apartheid** (*separation of the races*), another form of ethnic discrimination, was imposed on black South Africans by the white minority until 1990.

- **South Asia.** In South Asia, differences between Hindus and Muslims led to the partition of British India into India and Pakistan in 1947. Clashes between Pakistan and India, especially over the future of Kashmir, continue to cloud the future. Recently there has been periodic violence between between Hindus and Sikhs, and the assassination of several Indian leaders.

- **Eastern Europe.** Ethnic differences between Czechs and Slovaks led to the division of Czechoslovakia in 1991. In the former Yugoslavia, ethnic rivalries between Orthodox Christian Serbs, Catholic Croats, and Muslim Bosnians led to the dissolution of the country and a bitter civil war in which some groups, especially the Serbs, tried to eliminate other groups through "**ethnic cleansing**." More recently, Serbs have been accused of atrocities against Albanians in Kosovo.

- **Western Europe.** In Northern Ireland, disagreements between Protestants and Catholics have led to decades of violence. Elsewhere, large numbers of Turkish, North African, and Pakistani workers have flooded Western Europe in search of jobs. These "guest workers" are not always welcomed by Europeans.

STATUS OF WOMEN

World processes like urbanization, global communication, and economic development have greatly affected the status of women in many cultures. In many traditional societies, women were considered inferior and men held most decision-making powers. With the Industrial Revolution, more women entered the workforce. In industrialized societies, women's and men's perceptions, especially about the role of women in society, began to change. Women slowly began to be seen as the equals of men. After World War I, women in many industrialized societies won the right to vote. Yet women still have an inferior status in many parts of the world today. In some Islamic countries, for example, women cannot drive cars or make public appearances without wearing a veil.

SECTION 2 — MAJOR GEOGRAPHIC TERMS AND CONCEPTS

Terms and concepts are important to the study of geography. Use the following graphic organizer to see how many you can recall.

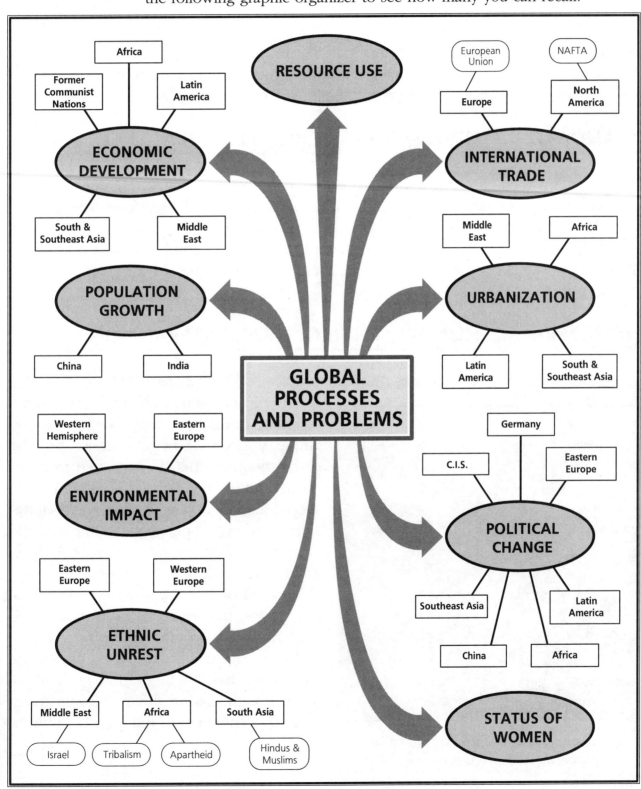

SECTION 3 · THE CONTENT STANDARDS FOR GEOGRAPHY

In Chapter 4, you learned that its not possible to answer High School Test questions correctly simply by understanding the prompt. Prompts are used to test your knowledge of the content standards. This section explains the content standards for geography.

STANDARD II.1: DIVERSITY OF PEOPLE, PLACES, AND CULTURES

This standard focuses on how world events and problems affect various peoples and societies in different ways. For example, high oil prices would affect countries that sell and those that buy oil differently. You should also be able to explain how cultural factors help shape the perceptions of women and men. For example, women in Western Europe and China often assume roles outside the home that would not be permitted in Saudi Arabia.

STANDARD II.2: HUMAN / ENVIRONMENT INTERACTION

This standard looks at interactions between people and their physical environment. You should be able to describe the environmental effects of major world processes. For example, you should be able to describe the global warming that has resulted from industrialization and population growth. You should also be able to explain the relationship between property ownership and the management of natural resources. For example, some Middle Eastern countries are able to sell oil because they own the property where this resource is located. Similarly, Brazil controls the Amazon rain forest, and therefore has been able to permit the large-scale harvesting of timber there — even though cutting down the rain forest may be detrimental to the world's environment.

Millions of hardwood trees like these have been cut down in the Amazon rain forest

STANDARD II.3: LOCATION, MOVEMENT, AND CONNECTIONS

This standard examines world economic activities and global interdependence. You should be able to locate and describe major world patterns of economic activity and explain the reasons for these patterns. For example, Japan imports natural resources like oil and exports manufactured products like cars. This is because Japan lacks many natural resources, but has a highly skilled and educated workforce, and its government policies support research and advanced technology. You should also be able to explain how various current events have both causes and effects in other parts of the world.

STANDARD II.4: REGIONS, PATTERNS, AND PROCESSES

This standard focuses on the concept of region. You should be able to explain how major world processes like urbanization, economic growth, global trade, communication, population growth, and improvements in information technology are affecting different world regions. You should also be able to explain how major world regions, like Africa, the Middle East, China, or Latin America are changing. You should further be able to describe major patterns of economic development and political systems and explain how they came about.

A clerk waits on customers in China, where free markets are developing

For example, you should be able to identify China as having a Communist government and a growing number of private businesses. Africa was dependent on trade with Europe for industrial goods during the colonial period, but since that time has been developing its own industries.

Students at the Hotel and Tourism Training Center in Tanzania

STANDARD II.5: GLOBAL ISSUES AND EVENTS

This standard requires you to stay informed about current events and to understand their connections to world geography. You should be able to describe events taking place in various world regions, such as the way in which disputes have arisen among some nations for control of regional resources. You should know how these events are influenced by geography and major world processes. Lastly, you should be able to explain the causes of global issues and their importance, such as the struggles among various ethnic groups in Bosnia and Kosovo.

PRACTICE QUESTIONS

This section starts with two clusters of practice selected-response questions. This section also contains two constructed-response questions. Each one has a prompt and a writing task related to it. Examine each prompt carefully and write your answers as directed. Each question has a benchmark number to indicate which content standard is being tested. A list of the geography benchmarks is at the end of this chapter.

— CLUSTERS OF SELECTED-RESPONSE QUESTIONS —

Directions: Examine the following table and map and use them with what you already know to answer the questions that follow.

COMPARING NATIONS (1997)

Category	Country A	Country B	Country C	Country D	Country E
Yearly Increase in Population	0.6%	1.2%	0.2%	1.9%	2.3%
Per Capita Income (in U.S. dollars)	$27,607	$5,580	$18,670	$950	$22,480
Infant Mortality	15 per 1,000	55 per 1,000	6 per 1,000	119 per 1,000	20 per 1,000
Life Expectancy	76 years	62 years	79 years	40 years	73 years
Literacy Rate	96%	83%	99%	61%	79%
Labor Force	56% service 26% industr. 6% finance 2% agricult.	42% service 31% agricult. 27% indust.	62% service 31% indust. 7% agricult.	93% agricult.	85% indust. 5% service 5% agricult. 5% gov't.

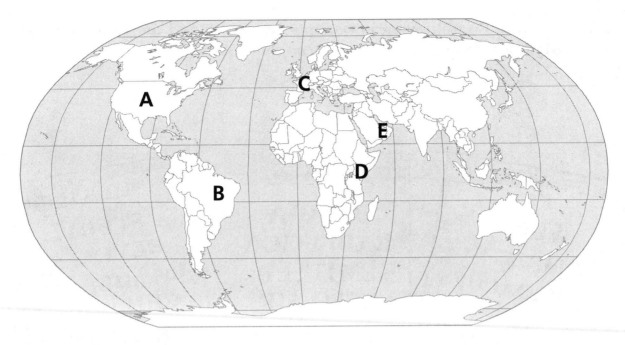

1 According to the data, which statement would BEST explain the per capita income of Country E?

  A It has vast oil reserves which are in demand throughout the world.
  B It is a major agricultural nation, exporting crops world-wide.
  C It has many of the largest universities in the world.
  D Its climate is extremely suitable for agriculture.

II.3.HS.1

2 Which nation would MOST likely be classified as a developing nation?

  A Country A   **C** Country D
  B Country C   **D** Country E

II.5.HS.2

3 Which nation MOST likely spends the LEAST amount of money on social services for its people?

  A Country A   **C** Country D
  B Country C   **D** Country E

II.5.HS.2

4 According to the data, which two countries MOST likely have the highest percentage of people attending college?

  A Country A and Country E
  B Country C and Country D
  C Country D and Country E
  D Country A and Country C

II.1.HS.2

5 Damage to the natural resources of which two nations would PROBABLY cause the most worldwide environmental concern?

  A Country D and Country E
  B Country C and Country D
  C Country B and Country E
  D Country C and Country E

II.2.HS.1

Name _____ Teacher_____

Directions: Read the following newspaper headlines and use them with what you already know to answer the questions that follow.

NEW YORK TRIBUNE

WORLD
POPULATION
APPROACHES
SIX
BILLION
PEOPLE

RUSSIAN GAZETTE

DEADLY
RADIATION
EMITTED
INTO AIR
AT
CHERNOBYL

UNITED NATIONS WORLD BULLETIN

STUDY
REVEALS
150 MILLION
CHILDREN
GO TO BED
HUNGRY
EACH NIGHT

WORLD PRESS

LOSS OF
RAIN FORESTS
THREATENS
SOME
SPECIES
WITH
EXTINCTION

AFRICAN HERALD

UNEMPLOYMENT
CONTINUES
TO RISE
AS
NATIONS
INCREASE
AUTOMATION

RWANDA JOURNAL

CITIES
UNABLE TO
HANDLE
POPULATION
SHIFT TO
URBAN
CENTERS

6 Which title BEST summarizes the main idea behind these headlines?

A Concerns of Developing Nations
B Problems Facing the United States Today
C International Problems and Concerns
D Environmental Problems Around the Globe

II.1.HS.1

7 Which two newspaper headlines are MOST concerned with the dangers of global environmental damage?

A *African Herald* and *U.N. World Bulletin*
B *Rwanda Journal* and *New York Tribune*
C *World Press* and *Russian Gazette*
D *New York Tribune* and *African Herald*

II.2.HS.1

8 In which two newspapers would the headline most likely be tied to an editorial about birth control?

A *Rwanda Journal* and *New York Tribune*
B *World Press* and *Russian Gazette*
C *Rwanda Journal* and *Russian Gazette*
D *New York Tribune* and *African Herald*

II.5.HS.2

9 The headline in the *U.N. World Bulletin* MOST likely focuses on concerns facing which two nations?

A Canada and India
B France and Mexico
C Somalia and Indonesia
D Australia and Japan

II.4.HS.3

10
• **Increased Pollution Due to Traffic Congestion**
• **Health Dangers Posed by Increase of Sewage**
• **Acute Shortage of Housing Develops**

The three sub-headlines above would MOST likely accompany the headline found in which newspaper?

A *African Herald*
B *Rwanda Journal*
C *World Press*
D *Russian Gazette*

II.5.HS.2

Name _____ Teacher _____

— CONSTRUCTED-RESPONSE QUESTIONS —

Following are two constructed-response questions. Read the directions and examine each question carefully before answering. Each question has a benchmark number to show you which content standard is being tested.

Directions: You should take about 5 minutes to examine the following political cartoon and use it with what you already know to complete this task.

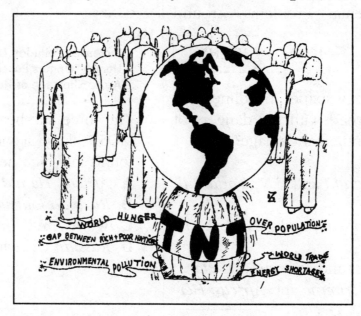

11 On the lines provided, explain the cause of **one** problem indicated in the cartoon and **explain how** it became a world problem.

Cause of the problem: _____

How it became a world problem: _____

_____

_____

_____

_____

II.1.HS.1

Name _____ Teacher_____

Directions: You should take about 5 minutes to examine the following diagram and use it with what you already know to complete this task.

12 On the lines provided, select **one** global development from the diagram above and **show how** this development is affecting at least two regions of the world.

Identification and explanation of how a major global development is affecting one

world region: _____

_____

_____

_____

Identification and explanation of how this development is affecting a second world

region: _____

_____

_____

_____

II.4.HS.3

Name _____   Teacher _____

BENCHMARKS OF THE GEOGRAPHY STRAND

Standard II.1: Diversity of People, Places, and Cultures

II.1.HS.1 Describe how major world issues and events affect various people, societies, places, and cultures in different ways.

II.1.HS.2 Explain how culture might affect women's and men's perceptions.

Standard II.2: Human/Environment Interaction

II.2.HS.1 Describe the environmental consequences of major world processes and events.

II.2.HS.2 Assess the relationship between property ownership and the management of natural resources.

Standard II.3: Location, Movement, and Connections

II.3.HS.1 Describe the major world patterns of economic activity and explain the reasons for the patterns.

II.3.HS.2 Explain how events have causes and consequences in different parts of the world.

Standard II.4: Regions, Patterns, and Processes

II.4.HS.1 Explain how major world processes affect different world regions.

II.4.HS.2 Explain how major world regions are changing.

II.4.HS.3 Explain how processes like population growth, economic development, urbanization resource use, international trade, global communication, and environmental impact are affecting different world regions.

II.4.HS.4 Describe major patterns of economic development and political systems and explain some of the factors causing them.

Standard II.5: Global Issues and Events

II.5.HS.1 Explain how geography and major world processes influence major world events.

II.5.HS.2 Explain the causes and importance of global issues involving cultural stability and change, economic development and international trade, resource use, environmental impact, conflict and cooperation, and explain how they may affect the future.

General Sherman and staff during the Civil War

The Great Depression caused devastating poverty

Astronaut "Buzz" Aldrin about to step onto the moon

A CAPSULE SUMMARY OF HISTORY

The following summary will help you recall important information to prepare you for the High School Test in Social Studies.

THE NATURE OF HISTORY

Historians are concerned with understanding and explaining past events and ways of life. Historians depend upon two kinds of sources to learn about the past:

✦ **Primary Sources** are original records of an event or way of life that is under investigation. Primary sources include artifacts, eyewitness reports, official records from the time of the event, letters sent by people involved in the event, and photographs. For example, a diary written by an abolitionist in the period leading to the Civil War would be a primary source. All historical facts used to reconstruct past events can be traced back to primary sources.

✦ **Secondary Sources** are the writings and interpretations of historians and other writers. Secondary sources such as textbooks and articles often provide convenient summaries of information originally found in primary sources.

THE EARLY NINETEENTH CENTURY, 1815-1850

From the end of the War of 1812 to the eve of the Civil War, the United States became more democratic, expanded westward, and laid the foundation for its future foreign policy.

✦ **The Monroe Doctrine.** Most of Latin America successfully rebelled from Spanish rule during this period. President James Monroe issued the Monroe Doctrine, stating that the United States would oppose any attempt by European nations to establish new colonies or to reconquer old ones in the Western Hemisphere.

✦ **Jacksonian Democracy. Andrew Jackson** was elected President in 1828. Jackson was the first President not born to wealth. His time in office was accompanied by many democratic reforms. States eliminated property qualifications, allowing all adult white males to vote. Jackson filled many public offices with his supporters under the **spoils system**, based on the view that it was good to change office holders and give ordinary citizens experience in government.

◆ **Westward Expansion**. The completion of the **Erie Canal** greatly helped the settlement of the Midwest. Settlers filled the lands of the Northwest Territory, which now became states. Michigan was admitted as a state in 1837. Many Americans came to believe it was America's **Manifest Destiny** to expand the nation to the shores of the Pacific. One such opportunity came when settlers in the Mexican province of Texas declared independence and defeated Mexican forces in 1836. In 1845, the U.S. Congress voted to annex Texas. A dispute between the United States and Mexico over the Texas border led to the **Mexican-American War** (1846-1848). After the United States won the war, Mexico was forced to cede the territory now occupied by California, Nevada, Utah, Arizona, and parts of Colorado and New Mexico.

CIVIL WAR AND RECONSTRUCTION, 1850-1877

The Civil War was the bloodiest war in American history. It had many causes:

◆ **Sectionalism**. As the United States grew, each region developed its own characteristics. The **Northeast** became a center of manufacturing, shipping, fishing, and small farms. Most Southerners did not own slaves. However, much of the **South's** economy was based on profits from using slave labor on large plantations to grow cash crops like cotton for sale to England or the Northeast. The **Midwestern** states became nation's breadbasket, growing and shipping grain to the Northeast and South.

◆ **Slavery**. The invention of the cotton gin increased the demand for slave labor in the South. At the same time, **abolitionists** were attempting to end slavery. Many slaves escaped through the **Underground Railroad**.

◆ **States' Rights**. Many Southerners believed that each state had the power to reject federal law in its own territory or to leave the Union altogether if it wished.

Harriet Beecher Stowe's novel Uncle Tom's Cabin *helped spread moral outrage against slavery.*

◆ **Western Expansion**. As the United States expanded westward, new states were added to the Union. This posed the problem of whether the new states should enter the Union as slave or free states.

The Civil War Begins. The **Republican Party** was formed to oppose the spread of slavery to new territories. In 1860, **Abraham Lincoln**, the Republican candidate, was elected President. Southern states, fearing Lincoln would abolish slavery, seceded from the Union and formed the **Confederate States of America**.

Lincoln resolved to preserve the unity of the nation. When the Confederates fired on **Fort Sumter**, a federal fort in South Carolina, the Civil War officially began.

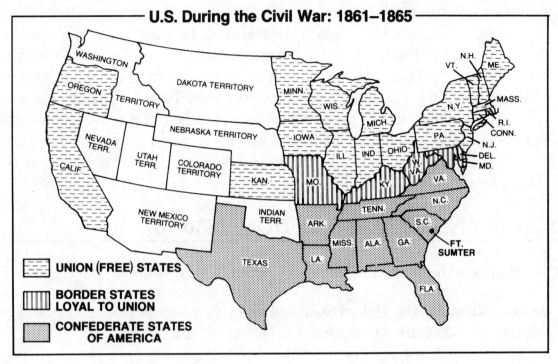

U.S. During the Civil War: 1861–1865

UNION (FREE) STATES

BORDER STATES LOYAL TO UNION

CONFEDERATE STATES OF AMERICA

Fighting in the Civil War. The North eventually triumphed because of its larger population, better transportation, superior industry, and greater naval power. Lincoln freed the slaves in the South with the **Emancipation Proclamation** (1862). The **Thirteenth Amendment** (1865) abolished slavery throughout the United States.

Aftermath of the Civil War. When the war ended in 1865, the South was in shambles — cities, railroad lines, and plantations had been destroyed by Union armies. Plantations no longer had slaves, and the freed slaves, known as **freedmen**, lacked jobs, land, and income.

Reconstruction. The Reconstruction Period (1865-1877) refers to the decade after the Civil War. When Lincoln was assassinated in 1865, **Andrew Johnson** became President. Johnson attempted to readmit Southern states to the Union on lenient terms. Southern states, however, were slow to extend voting rights to the freedmen. They also passed **Black Codes** which restricted the movements of the former slaves. The **Radical Republicans** in Congress refused to recognize these new state governments in the South. Instead, they imposed military rule and passed a Civil Rights Act giving freedmen full rights. The latter act became the basis for the **Fourteenth Amendment**, which declared that no state government could deny American citizens full rights or equality before the law. Southern ratification of the new amendment became a condition for readmission to the Union. When Johnson opposed Congressional reconstruction plans, he was impeached. During Johnson's impeachment trial, the Senate failed — by only one vote — to remove him from office.

The Reconstruction Governments. Former Confederates were barred from voting or holding office. Instead, freedmen and so-called **carpetbaggers** and **scalawags** held power. Reconstruction governments built new schools, roads, and railroads, and banned racial discrimination. To deal with economic problems, plantation owners and freedmen developed the system of **sharecropping**. Former plantation owners provided livestock, tools, and land to former slaves in exchange for a share of the crop.

Reconstruction Ends. Reconstruction ended when Northern troops were withdrawn in 1877. Former Confederate leaders returned to power, and freedmen lost most of their new rights. The **Ku Klux Klan** terrorized Southern blacks who challenged white control. Southern state governments passed **Jim Crow** laws, segregating whites from blacks in schools and other public facilities. These laws were upheld by the U.S. Supreme Court in the case of ***Plessy v. Ferguson*** (1896). In the late 19th and early 20th centuries, African-American leaders such as **Booker T. Washington** and **W.E.B. DuBois** spoke out against these injustices.

In 1909, W.E.B. DuBois helped found the NAACP.

THE RISE OF INDUSTRY AND CHANGING AMERICAN LIFE-STYLES, 1865-1890

In the years after the Civil War, the United States became one of the world's leading industrial nations. Many factors help explain this growth:

✦ **Railroads**. The number of railroads greatly increased. They made it possible to move food from farms to cities, and manufactured goods from one part of the country to another.

✦ **Population Growth**. A rising population was a major factor behind industrialization. The nation's population doubled between 1860 and 1900. This growth provided more people to make and buy goods and services.

✦ **Technology**. New inventions such as the sewing machine, typewriter, telephone, and the electric light bulb helped to stimulate further growth.

Completion of the transcontinental railroad in 1869 encouraged development of the West.

Rise of Big Business. People developed new ways to organize businesses, allowing them to raise larger sums of money. Corporations, in which stockholders invested their money, became prevalent. Entrepreneurs like **Andrew Carnegie** *(steel)* and **John D. Rockefeller** *(oil)*, developed large businesses which came to dominate entire industries.

Rise of Labor Unions. The growth of industry and big business helped the country in many ways, but sometimes led to problems like the abuse of workers or unfair competition. To improve their working conditions and increase wages, workers organized into labor unions. Unions attempted **collective bargaining** with employers and went on strike to get employers to meet their demands. Two important national workers' organizations were the **Knights of Labor** and the **American Federation of Labor** (A.F.L.).

The Consequences of Industrialization. The expansion of American industry affected almost every aspect of American life.

In tenement buildings like these, many immigrant families often crowded into one apartment.

◆ **Urbanization**. People flocked to cities in search of work and new opportunities. Often cities were ill prepared for so many people, lacking adequate public services like hospitals, police, fire protection, schools, and garbage collection. Families lived in crowded and unhealthy tenement buildings.

◆ **Immigration**. One reason cities grew so fast was because of immigration. Factories, railroads, and mines needed large numbers of workers. Unlike past immigrants, most newcomers settled in cities and were unable to speak English. These immigrants were opposed by **nativists**, who wanted immigration to be slowed down or stopped. Eventually, legislation was passed restricting immigration after World War I.

◆ **Women's Roles.** Women were also affected by industrialization. At the time, most women had few rights — they could not vote, serve on juries, or hold public office. This started to change in the late 19th century. Small numbers of women began going to college. Leaders such as **Elizabeth Cady Stanton** and **Susan B. Anthony** started the **Suffrage Movement** to win the right to vote for women.

◆ **Settlement of the Last Frontier.** Between 1860 and 1890, railroads were built across the Great Plains and Far West. Cowboys drove cattle across the open range to railroad lines. The **Homestead Act** enabled settlers to claim government land if they farmed it for five years. Cattle and wheat from the Central Lowlands and Great Plains were shipped to cities to feed laborers.

✦ **Plight of Native Americans**. As settlers pushed westward, huge herds of buffalo were destroyed. After a series of conflicts on the frontier in the 1870s and 1880s, Native Americans in the Great Plains and Far West were pushed onto reservations.

THE PROGRESSIVE ERA, 1890-1920

The transformation of America into an industrial nation created many problems. These led to an age of reform known as the Progressive Era.

The Grange Movement. Farmers faced great difficulties when the opening of the West and the construction of railroads made more crops available. Over-production led to falling crop prices, while production costs remained high. Many farmers fell into debt. Blaming railroads and the gold standard for their difficulties, farmers formed the Grange Movement to overcome these problems.

The Populist Party. Farmers soon joined with laborers to form the Populist Party in 1892. Populists believed banks, railroads, and Big Business held too much power. Populist leaders proposed a secret ballot, direct election of Senators, a graduated income tax, and the unlimited coinage of silver to raise farm prices. In 1896, the Democratic candidate for President, **William Jennings Bryan**, adopted much of the Populist platform but lost the election. Bryan lost again in 1900.

The Progressive Movement. The Progressive Movement emerged around 1900. Progressives were primarily middle-class and urban. They were outraged at government corruption and the conditions of the urban poor, and wanted government to correct these abuses. Among the Progressives were a group of newspaper reporters known as **muckrakers**. They exposed dishonest politicians and business leaders as well as the sufferings of the poor. Some of the most famous muckrakers were Upton Sinclair, Jacob Riis, and Ida Tarbell. Presidents **Theodore Roosevelt** (1901-1909) and **Woodrow Wilson** (1913-1921) introduced many Progressive reforms. Roosevelt protected consumers with the **Meat Inspection Act** and the **Pure Food and Drug Act**. He formed the Natural Conservation Commission to protect the environment, and broke up large monopolies like the Standard Oil Company. Wilson lowered tariffs and passed the graduated income tax (1913), which allowed the federal government to collect taxes directly from individuals. He also helped pass the **Federal Reserve Act** (1913) to control the nation's money supply.

Teddy Roosevelt (4th from left) in front of a giant redwood tree

American Foreign Policy in the Progressive Era. In the Progressive Era, Americans became more involved in world affairs.

✦ **The Spanish-American War (1898)**. In the 1890s, Cubans rebelled against Spain to obtain independence. American newspapers sensationalized incidents of Spanish brutality in putting down the rebellion. When the U.S. battleship *Maine* blew up in Havana harbor, the American press blamed Spain and President McKinley declared war. The U.S. won the war and took the Philippines, Guam, and Puerto Rico as colonies. Officially, Cuba became independent, but in reality it came under U.S. control.

✦ **American Imperialism**. In 1904, President Roosevelt announced the Roosevelt Corollary to the Monroe Doctrine, or **Big Stick Policy**. It stated that the United States would act as policeman to the Western Hemisphere, and would not allow European intervention there. In Panama, Roosevelt backed rebels declaring their independence from Colombia, so that the United States could acquire the right to build the **Panama Canal**, linking the Atlantic to the Pacific Ocean. The United States also annexed Hawaii and Samoa, and announced the **Open Door Policy** (1899), stating that all nations should have commercial rights in China.

World War I. In 1914, war broke out among the great powers of Europe. Great Britain, France, and Russia *(the Allies)* opposed Germany, Austria-Hungary, and Ottoman Turkey *(the Central Powers)*. When German submarines attacked American ships in

EUROPE AT THE START OF WORLD WAR I

The Allies
The Central Powers

1917, the United States declared war to protect freedom of the seas. American intervention helped break the deadlock in Europe, and by November 1918 Germany surrendered. President Woodrow Wilson announced America's war aims in the **Fourteen**

Points, which stated that each nationality should have its own nation-state, and that all nations should unite in a **League of Nations** to prevent future aggression. But Americans had become disillusioned and retreated into **isolationism**. The U.S. Senate rejected the Treaty of Versailles, and the United States never joined the League of Nations.

PROSPERITY, DEPRESSION, AND WAR, 1920-1945

In the quarter of a century from 1920 to 1945, Americans faced two of the most serious crises in their history — an economic depression and a global war.

The Roaring Twenties. For many Americans, the 1920s were good times. Wages rose and job opportunities increased, while business profits and production soared. There were many factors underlying this prosperity:

♦ **Rise of the Automobile**. American ownership of automobiles tripled, stimulating related industries like steel, glass, and rubber.

♦ **The Age of Mass Consumption**. Higher wages, more advertising, and the availability of new products like cars, radios, and refrigerators led people to buy more.

♦ **Republican Business Policies**. A series of Republican Presidents followed pro-business policies such as high tariffs, lower taxes on the wealthy and corporations, and lax enforcement of the anti-trust laws *(laws against unfair business practices)*. President Coolidge announced that "the business of America is business."

Changes in Social Patterns and Cultural Values. The greater mobility and comforts of the 1920s had a strong impact on social patterns and cultural values. Women, African Americans, and the young felt a new sense of freedom and power. Women won the right to vote with the **Nineteenth Amendment** (1920). They began wearing shorter hair and shorter dresses, emphasizing their mobility and equality. African Americans migrated to Northern cities in large numbers. Langston Hughes, Countee Culleen, and Alain Locke expressed a new pride in their heritage, helping to launch the **Harlem Renaissance**. Jazz music, with its origins in black spirituals and blues, gained popularity.

The Great Depression. Prosperity led to increasing speculation on the New York Stock Exchange. In October 1929, the Stock Market crashed when prices fell dramatically. After the crash, corporations found it hard to raise money and many went out of

Droughts and wind turned the Great Plains into a "Dust Bowl" during the Great Depression.

business. People who had borrowed money to buy stocks could not repay their loans, leading to many bank failures. Millions of people lost their jobs and homes. The Great Depression was one of the worst economic disasters in American history. The Depression spread to Europe when American bankers tried to call in overseas loans.

Franklin Roosevelt and the New Deal. President Herbert Hoover introduced some relief measures, but they were too little, too late. In the 1932 election, Democratic candidate **Franklin D. Roosevelt** was elected after promising Americans a "**New Deal**." Roosevelt quickly introduced many new measures aimed at "Relief, Recovery, and Reform."

Roosevelt (seated) signing the law creating federal bank deposit insurance

✦ **Relief** measures were steps to help people in the short term. The federal government provided jobs improving the land or building public works in the **Civilian Conservation Corps**, **Public Works Administration**, and other new agencies.

✦ **Recovery** programs helped stimulate and control production. The **Agricultural Adjustment Act** (1933) aided farmers by limiting production. The **National Recovery Administration** (1933) drew up codes for businesses, but was later declared unconstitutional by the Supreme Court.

✦ **Reform** measures sought to correct the flaws in the economy that had caused the Great Depression to begin. The **Social Security Act** (1935) insured people against unemployment and provided modest retirement benefits. The **Wagner Act** (1935) guaranteed workers the right to join a labor union.

The New Deal vs. the U.S. Supreme Court. The New Deal was extremely popular among Americans, but the Supreme Court ruled that several of its programs were unconstitutional. President Roosevelt threatened to appoint more justices to "pack" the Court. Roosevelt eventually backed down, but the Supreme Court stopped overturning New Deal legislation.

The U.S. Enters World War II. The Great Depression and the New Deal came to an end when the United States again became involved in a world war. In Europe, the Depression had helped bring dictators like Adolf Hitler to power. World War II began when Germany invaded Poland in 1939. The Germans quickly conquered France and much of Europe. Congress passed the **Neutrality Acts** to keep the United States out of the war. Then on December 7, 1941, Japanese planes attacked the U.S. Pacific Fleet at

U.S.S. Shaw bombed at Pearl Harbor

Pearl Harbor, Hawaii. The United States declared war on Japan, while Germany and Italy declared war on the United States.

The Home Front. America concentrated its efforts on winning the war in Europe first. Fifteen million men enlisted or were drafted during the war. American factories quickly switched from consumer goods to military production, and women took factory jobs. One effect of the war was the forced relocation of many innocent Japanese-Americans, upheld by the Supreme Court in ***Korematsu v. United States*** (1944).

Allied Victory. Germany invaded the Soviet Union in 1941, but the bitter cold of the Russian winter and Soviet military resistance gradually pushed the Germans back. In 1944, British and American troops landed in France on **D-Day**. By May 1945, Germany was occupied by Allied forces and surrendered. Allied forces also liberated the concentration camps where the Nazis had murdered millions of Jews and other innocent people in the **Holocaust**. A few months later, Japan surrendered after the United States dropped its new weapon, the atomic bomb, on the cities of Hiroshima and Nagasaki.

The atomic bomb dropped on Nagasaki

AMERICA IN UNCERTAIN TIMES, 1945-1965

In the post-war years, Americans enjoyed greater prosperity than ever before, while the U.S. took a dominant role in world affairs. Nevertheless, these were times of tremendous uncertainty. The U.S. became involved in a deadly contest with the Soviet Union abroad, while at home steps were finally taken to end centuries of racial injustice.

The Emergence of the Cold War. The roots of the **Cold War** lay in the differences between two political and economic systems — the democratic, capitalist system of the United States and the totalitarian, Communist system of the Soviet Union. Each country looked with suspicion and alarm at attempts by the other to spread its beliefs.

The Cold War in Europe. The Soviet dictator, **Joseph Stalin**, created a Soviet sphere of influence in Eastern Europe. President Truman was outraged when Stalin violated his promise to hold free elections in Eastern European countries. When Communist rebels appeared to threaten Greece and Turkey in 1947, Truman announced the **Truman Doctrine**, which stated that America would give assistance to any government resisting Communism. Soon afterwards, Truman also announced the **Marshall Plan**, a program of massive economic aid to help Europeans rebuild their war-torn economies.

The Division of Germany and the Creation of NATO. After World War II, Germany was divided into four Allied occupation zones. As a result of the Cold War, the western zones were merged into West Germany, while the Soviet zone became the Communist nation of East Germany. Berlin, the former German capital, was similarly divided between East and West. When Stalin attempted to cut off West Berlin from the West, the Western Allies began a massive airlift to feed and supply the city. After one year, Stalin finally lifted the blockade.

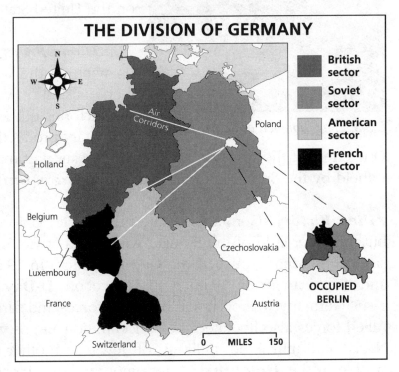

In response to these tensions, the United States, Canada, and ten Western European nations formed the **North Atlantic Treaty Organization (NATO)** in 1949. The purpose of NATO was primarily to protect Western Europe from Communist aggression. The Soviet Union responded several years later by forming the **Warsaw Pact**, an alliance of Eastern European countries under Soviet control.

The Cold War Spreads to Asia. Just when Americans believed they had succeeded in containing Communism in Europe, it spread to Asia.

✦ **China**. The world's most populous nation fell to Communism in 1949. The Nationalist Chinese fled to the island of Taiwan, where they claimed to be the legitimate government of China.

✦ **Korea**. Communist North Korea invaded South Korea in 1950. President Truman resolved to resist this aggression and ordered U.S. forces into South Korea. The United Nations sent additional troops to support the South Koreans. A truce between North and South Korea was finally signed in 1953, which left the country divided exactly as it had been before the war.

The Cold War at Home. The rise of the Cold War, the fall of China, and the spread of nuclear weapons to the Soviet Union led to increased fears of Communism at home. In 1950 Senator **Joseph McCarthy** shocked the nation by claiming to know the names of hundreds of Communists who worked in the U.S. government. The U.S. Congress began investigating many prominent people for "un-American" activities.

The Civil Rights Movement. The most important domestic development in the late 1950s and early 1960s was the Civil Rights Movement. During World War II, more than one million African Americans had served in the armed forces. Many of them now demanded equality at home. America's role as a symbol of freedom on the world stage further encouraged their claims for equal rights.

◆ **Brown v. Board of Education (1954)**. In this important court case, NAACP lawyers, led by **Thurgood Marshall**, challenged segregated public schools for denying African-American children "equal protection of the law," as required by the Fourteenth Amendment. The Supreme Court, led by Chief Justice **Earl Warren**, ruled that racial segregation in public schools was unconstitutional.

◆ **Montgomery Bus Boycott**. African Americans and their sympathizers organized to challenge segregation in other areas. **Rosa Parks** began the Montgomery Bus Boycott in Alabama (1955-1956) when she refused to sit in the back of a public bus. Other African Americans staged sit-ins at "whites only" lunch counters, and held marches and demonstrations.

Rosa Parks

◆ **Dr. Martin Luther King, Jr.** Dr. King emerged as the leader of the Civil Rights Movement. King believed the best way to fight racism was through non-violent civil disobedience. Arrested in Alabama in 1963, King wrote a letter from jail explaining the need for African Americans to stand up for their rights. Later that same year, King organized a massive **March on Washington**, where he gave his famous **"I Have A Dream" Speech**.

President Johnson Pushes for Change. As a result of the Civil Rights Movement, President Lyndon Johnson pushed the **Civil Rights Act** (1964) through Congress. This law prohibited racial discrimination in hotels, restaurants, unions, and businesses engaged in interstate commerce. The following year, Congress passed the **Voting Rights**

Dr. King and his followers during the March on Washington, 1963

Act, which prevented states from denying African Americans the right to vote. President Johnson also began the first **Affirmative Action** programs, requiring institutions and businesses doing business with the federal government to hire more minority and female employees to correct past imbalances.

THE LIMITS OF POWER, 1965-1975

In the 1960s and 1970s, Americans learned that despite their unparalleled economic and military strength, there were limits to American power.

The Kennedy Presidency (1961-1963). In 1960, John F. Kennedy was elected President. Kennedy gave his support to the Civil Rights Movement, and initiated the "space race" when he proposed to land the first person on the moon. Kennedy also continued to struggle with Cold War problems. The Cold War reached the Western Hemisphere when **Fidel Castro** established a Communist government in Cuba in 1959. Anti-Castro Cubans, trained in the United States, invaded Cuba at the **Bay of Pigs** in 1961. The invasion failed, in part because Kennedy refused to provide U.S. air support.

The Cuban Missile Crisis. In 1962, Americans discovered that the Soviet Union was secretly installing nuclear missiles in Cuba aimed at the United States. During this crisis, Kennedy imposed a naval blockade on Cuba and threatened to invade the island. Soviet leader Nikita Khrushchev finally agreed to withdraw the missiles.

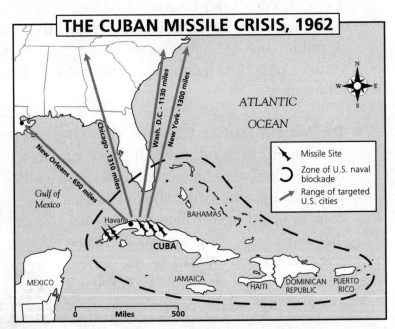

President Johnson and the Great Society. When Kennedy was assassinated in November 1963, Vice President Lyndon Johnson succeeded him as President. Johnson's **Great Society** legislation was the most ambitious social program since the New Deal. Johnson created **Medicare**, began a "**War on Poverty**," and increased federal aid to education and cities. By the late 1960s, however, these domestic programs were overshadowed by the Vietnam War.

The Vietnam War. In the early 1960s, Vietnamese Communists known as **Vietcong** launched a guerrilla war in South Vietnam. President Kennedy sent military advisers and economic aid to South Vietnam. In 1964, Congress passed the **Tonkin Gulf Resolution**, giving President Johnson authority to take emergency steps to stop a Communist takeover of South Vietnam. By 1967, over half a million U.S. soldiers were stationed there. Despite the large number of U.S. troops and superior weapons, the Americans and South Vietnamese made little headway against the Vietcong and North Vietnamese. As the prospect of victory faded, the war in Vietnam became one of the most unpopular in American history. Television brought the violence into American living rooms. Universities became centers of protest. The Anti-War Movement influenced the youth culture of the 1960s, in which many young people rebelled against the values of their elders. In addition, women began demanding greater equality in what became known as the **Women's Liberation Movement**.

Student burning his draft card (center) in one of many protests against the Vietnam War

The Nixon Presidency (1969-1974).

Richard Nixon was elected President in 1968 on the promise that he would achieve "**peace with honor**." He began withdrawing American troops but stepped up bombing of North Vietnam. In 1973, Nixon agreed to withdraw the remaining U.S. forces under the **Paris Peace Accords**. South Vietnam fell to North Vietnamese forces and the country was reunited under Communist control in 1975.

In his attempts to end the Vietnam War, President Nixon also launched a number of important foreign-policy moves. In 1972, he visited Communist China and restored normal diplomatic relations with that country. Nixon also became the first American President to visit Moscow, and reduced tensions with the Soviet Union through his policy of **détente**.

Despite these achievements, Nixon's Presidency was brought down by the **Watergate** scandal. Former government employees were caught breaking into Democratic Party headquarters. Nixon and his advisers tried to cover up the investigation of the break-in. Later, it was revealed that Nixon had tape-recorded his White House conversations. The Supreme Court ordered him to give the tapes to investigators. The tapes proved that he had used the power of the Presidency for an illegal cover-up. Facing impeachment, Nixon became the first President to resign.

The Ford Presidency (1974-1976).

Nixon was replaced by his Vice-President, Gerald Ford, a former Congressman from Michigan. One of Ford's first acts was to pardon Nixon, a step that was criticized by many. Ford's main concern was a troubled American economy. Because of sharply rising oil prices and the reduction of military spending at the end of the Vietnam War, the United States had a stagnant economy with high unemployment and high inflation — a combination known as **stagflation**.

President Gerald Ford

THE CONTEMPORARY UNITED STATES, 1976-PRESENT

The Carter Presidency (1976-1981). In 1976, Ford lost the Presidential election to Democrat Jimmy Carter. In domestic affairs, Carter created a Department of Energy and took steps to conserve the use of fuels, so that the United States would be less dependent on foreign oil supplies. In foreign policy, Carter wanted to provide moral leadership by championing human rights. He pressured the Soviet Union and other countries to grant human rights to their citizens, and severely cut U.S. aid to dictators. Carter signed the **Panama Canal Treaty** (1977), agreeing to eventually return the Panama Canal to Panama. His most noteworthy accomplishment was to bring the leaders of Israel and Egypt together to sign the **Camp David Accords** (1978), an important step towards peace in the Middle East.

President Carter (center) announces to Congress the details of the Camp David Accords.

During Carter's Presidency, Fundamentalist Muslims overthrew the pro-Western leader of Iran. **Ayatollah Khomeini**, Iran's new leader, broke off diplomatic relations with the United States. In 1979, Iranians seized 52 members of the U.S. Embassy in Teheran as hostages. Carter tried to free them, but his efforts failed. The hostages were finally released in 1981, just as Ronald Reagan was being sworn in as President.

The Reagan Presidency (1981-1989). President Reagan introduced far-reaching changes in both domestic and foreign policy. He reduced federal social programs and cut taxes on the wealthy to stimulate the economy, while borrowing heavily to increase military spending. As a result, the economy improved but the national debt doubled. In foreign affairs, Reagan took aggressive steps to contain Communist influence, such as aiding rebels in Afghanistan who were fighting Soviet troops. In his second term, Reagan became involved in the **Iran-Contra Affair**. It was revealed that his administration had sold arms to Iran and used the money illegally to aid the "Contras," a

President Reagan (second from right) meeting with his Cabinet

group trying to overthrow the government of Nicaragua. During his second term Reagan also held an important series of summit conferences with Soviet leader Mikhail Gorbachev, which led to the dismantling of thousands of nuclear weapons.

The Bush Presidency (1989-1993). George Bush was elected President in 1988. Much of his Presidency focused on foreign affairs. A series of momentous events occurred during his first two years in office. The countries of Eastern Europe were liberated from Communist domination, and Germany was reunified. Gorbachev's policies failed to solve the Soviet Union's severe economic problems, and many of the Soviet republics demanded independence. Under these pressures, the U.S.S.R. broke apart. After forty years, the Cold War was over.

New foreign challenges soon developed. In 1990, Bush sent U.S. armed forces to Saudi Arabia after Iraqi dictator **Saddam Hussein** conquered Kuwait. The next year, U.S. and allied forces expelled the Iraqis from Kuwait in the **Gulf War**. Despite his foreign policy successes, Bush faced a mounting budget deficit and an economic recession at home.

An American soldier stands atop a destroyed Iraqi tank. The oil fires in the background were set by the retreating Iraqis as an act of "ecoterrorism."

The Clinton Presidency (1993-present). Arkansas Governor Bill Clinton defeated George Bush in the 1992 election. Clinton promised an ambitious program of social reforms. Although his proposed health care plan was rejected by Congress, Clinton was able to increase taxes and reduce spending to cut the budget deficit. He also pushed the **North American Free Trade Agreement** (NAFTA) and a new crime bill through Congress, as well as a welfare reform package. Inflation and unemployment sank to new lows, while U.S. trade flourished. Clinton's domestic agenda suffered setbacks when Republicans took over Congress in the 1994 elections, but by 1998 the United States had a $70 billion budget surplus, its first in 25 years.

Bill Clinton being sworn in as President

In foreign policy, Clinton helped bring about a truce in the Bosnian civil war, deterred Serbian attacks on Albanians in Kosovo, and defused a crisis involving North Korea. He also advanced the Middle East peace process by persuading Israelis and Palestinians to sign a new agreement regarding the West Bank and security issues. Despite these successes, a scandal arising out of his affair with a White House intern threatened Clinton with impeachment in 1998.

SECTION 2

MAJOR HISTORICAL TERMS AND CONCEPTS

There are many important terms and concepts in history.
Use this graphic organizer to review their meanings.

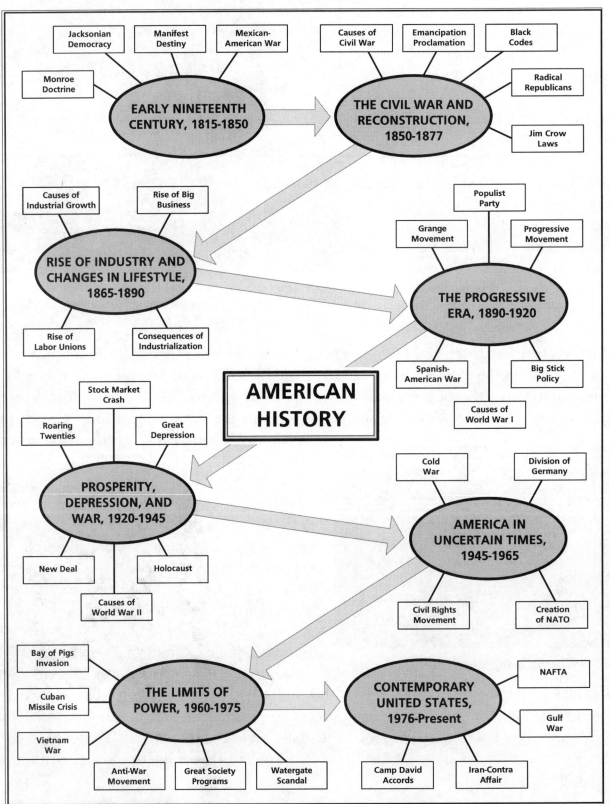

SECTION 3

THE CONTENT STANDARDS FOR HISTORY

In Chapter 4, you learned that you cannot answer High School Test questions correctly simply by interpreting the prompt. You must also understand the content standards. This section identifies Michigan's content standards for history.

STANDARD I.1: TIME AND CHRONOLOGY

This standard focuses on American history from 1815 to the present. You should be able to identify when major events occurred. You should also be able to interpret and construct timelines, showing both events and individuals. You should also know the chief factors characterizing the main eras of American and world history in this time span.

STANDARD I.2: COMPREHENDING THE PAST

This standard asks you to interpret narratives and graphic data describing significant events in U.S. history from 1815 to the present. You should also be able to identify key individuals from this period and be able to show how they were affected by their times, how they demonstrated good character, and how their achievements had a global impact.

STANDARD: I.3 ANALYZING AND INTERPRETING THE PAST

This standard focuses on how historians use primary and secondary sources to reconstruct past events. Historians often differ in their interpretations of the past. By comparing different interpretations, you should appreciate that our knowledge about the past is subject to change. You should be able to use both primary and secondary sources to analyze significant events in American history since 1815. For example, you should be able to explain how different choices in history might have led to different results. Finally, you should be able to take contemporary problems around the world today and trace the historical developments that led to those problems.

STANDARD: I.4 JUDGING DECISIONS FROM THE PAST

This standard asks you to identify and evaluate decisions from 1815 to the present in Michigan and the United States. You should be able to identify the factors that led to these major decisions, to consider alternative courses of action, and to evaluate these decisions in light of core democratic values. For example, what factors led to the New Deal? What alternative approaches could have been used to fight the Great Depression? What were the New Deal's advantages and disadvantages from the standpoints of workers, farmers, bankers, women, businessowners, and African Americans? Finally, you should be able to focus on individual responses to violations of human dignity, discrimination, and persecution in this period and in terms of costs and benefits from a variety of perspectives.

SECTION 4

PRACTICE QUESTIONS

This section contains practice selected-response and constructed-response questions about history. There are two clusters of selected-response questions. Each has a prompt and five questions. There are also two constructed-response questions, each with a prompt and a writing task. Each question has a benchmark number to indicate which benchmark is being tested. A list of the history benchmarks may be found at the end of this chapter.

— SELECTED-RESPONSE QUESTIONS —

Directions: Examine the following timeline and use it with what you already know to answer the questions that follow.

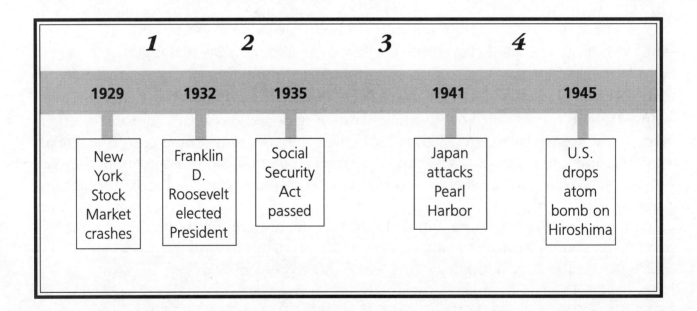

1 Which major event occurred during the same time period as the events listed on the timeline?

   A The Spanish-American War was fought.

   B Germany invaded Poland.

   C The Reconstruction Era ended.

   D The U.S. landed the first man on the moon.

   I.1.HS.2

2 Which title would be MOST appropriate for this timeline?

   A The Reconstruction Period

   B The Industrialization of Modern America

   C The Great Depression and World War II

   D Contemporary America

   I.1.HS.2

3 At what point on the timeline would you place British Prime Minister Neville Chamberlain's attempt to avoid war by meeting with Adolf Hitler in Munich?

   A Point 1

   B Point 2

   C Point 3

   D Point 4

   I.1.HS.1

4 Which person's achievements would MOST likely be placed on this timeline?

   A President Theodore Roosevelt

   B General Douglas MacArthur

   C President Woodrow Wilson

   D Senator Joseph McCarthy

   I.2.HS.3

5 Which U.S. Supreme Court decision is closely related to one of the events listed on the timeline?

   A *Marbury v. Madison*

   B *Brown v. Board of Education*

   C *Korematsu v. United States*

   D *Gideon v. Wainwright*

   I.1.HS.2

Name _____ Teacher _____

Directions: Read the following passage and use it with what you already know to answer the questions that follow.

DR. MARTIN LUTHER KING, JR.

In the 1950s and 1960s, the Civil Rights Movement struggled to end racial segregation. Dr. Martin Luther King, Jr., a Baptist minister, became one of the leaders of that movement.

King favored non-violent protest. If a government passed an unjust law, King believed people should oppose that law with non-violent actions such as marches and boycotts. He thought that peaceful resistance would eventually change other people's attitudes. King's tactics proved to be very effective against segregation.

Among King's greatest qualities was his personal courage. In organizing demonstrations in the South, he frequently risked imprisonment, violence and death. Enemies threatened King and his family. They tried to blow up his house. Still, he refused to give up.

One of King's most important demonstrations was a "March on Washington" in 1963. During this rally, King delivered a speech in which he told Americans of his dream of a nation free of prejudice and discrimination:

> *I have a dream. It is a dream deeply rooted in the American dream. I have a dream that one day this nation will rise up and live out the true meaning of its creed* [beliefs]: *We hold these truths to be self-evident, that all men are created equal. I have a dream that one day in the red hills of Georgia the sons of former slaves and the sons of former slave owners will be able to sit down together at the table of brotherhood.*

Dr. King helped end public segregation. The Civil Rights Act of 1964 banned segregation in public transportation, hotels and restaurants. King also fought to end unfair literacy *(reading)* tests and other requirements used to prevent African Americans from voting. Tragically, King was assassinated in 1968.

6 Which of the following would be a SECONDARY source you might consult to find out more about the central figure in this passage?

A The original draft of the "I Have A Dream" speech

B A newsreel of the March on Washington

C A biography of Dr. King

D Dr. King's letters to his wife

I.3.HS.1

7 Which *core democratic value* is referred to in Dr. King's speech in the passage?

A Justice

B Patriotism

C Popular sovereignty

D Checks and balances

I.4.HS.4

8 Which of the following events in U.S. history took place soon after the events discussed in this passage?

A The United States entered World War I.

B The Truman Doctrine was announced.

C The Vietnam War began.

D The Gulf War was fought.

I.1.HS.2

9 The ideas stated in the passage about ways of fighting oppression and inequality MOST closely resemble the ideas of which world figure?

A Mohandas Gandhi

B Joseph Stalin

C Mao Zedong

D Saddam Hussein

I.2.HS.3

10 Which U.S. Supreme Court decision mirrored many of the ideas expressed by King in the passage quoted?

A *Dred Scott*

B *Plessy v. Ferguson*

C *Brown v. Board of Education*

D *Miranda v. Arizona*

I.4.HS.2

Name _____ Teacher _____

— CONSTRUCTED-RESPONSE QUESTIONS —

Following are two constructed-response questions. Read the directions and examine each question carefully before answering. Each question has a benchmark number to show you which content standard is being tested.

Directions: You should take about 5 minutes to examine the following graphic organizer and use it with what you already know to complete this task.

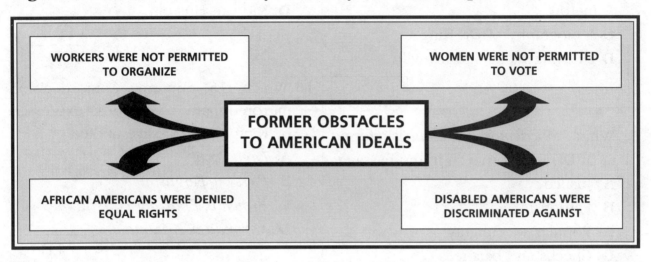

11 On the lines provided, identify **one** person and **show how** that person helped overcome one of the obstacles listed above.

Identification of person: _____

How that person helped overcome an obstacle to American ideals:_____

_____

_____

_____

_____

_____

_____

I.1.HS.2

Directions: You should take about 5 minutes to examine the following material and use it with what you already know to complete this task.

MAJOR EVENTS IN THE TWENTIETH CENTURY

Event 1
Mass Production
of Automobiles

Event 2
Amendment Giving
Women the Right to Vote

Event 3
Passage of the
Social Security Act

Event 4
Dropping of an Atom
Bomb on Hiroshima

Event 5
U.S. Withdrawal
from Vietnam

Event 6
Invention of
the Transistor

12 Certain key events in American history have had a world-wide impact. Such events may change the way people work, live, or think. On the lines provided, identify **one** event from the group shown above and **explain how** it has had a world-wide impact.

Identification of one of the above events: _____

_____

Explanation of how it has had a world-wide impact: _____

_____

_____

_____

_____

_____

_____

I.2.HS.2

Name _____ Teacher _____

BENCHMARKS OF THE HISTORY STRAND

Standard I.1: Time and Chronology

I.1.HS.1 Construct and interpret timelines of people and events in the history of Michigan and the United States since the Reconstruction era.

I.1.HS.2 Describe major factors that characterize the following eras in United States history: the development of the industrial United States (1870-1890), the emergence of modern America (1890-1930), the Great Depression and World War II (1929-1945), the post-war United States (1945-1970), and the contemporary United States (1968-present).

I.1.HS.3 Identify some of the major areas in world history and describe their defining characteristics.

Standard I.2: Comprehending The Past

I.2.HS.1 Draw upon narratives and graphic data to explain significant events that shaped the development of Michigan as a state and the United States as a nation during the eras since Reconstruction.

I.2.HS.2 Select events and individuals from the past that have had a global impact on the modern world and describe their impact.

I.2.HS.3 Identify and explain how individuals in history demonstrated good character and personal virtue.

Standard: I.3 Analyzing and Interpreting the Past

I.3.HS.1 Use primary and secondary records to analyze significant events that shaped the development of Michigan as a state and the United States as a nation since the era of Reconstruction.

I.3.HS.2 Challenge arguments of historical inevitability by formulating examples of how different choices could have led to different consequences.

I.3.HS.3 Select contemporary problems in the world and compose historical narratives that explain their antecedents.

Standard: I.4 Judging Decisions from the Past

I.4.HS.1 Identify major decisions in the history of Michigan and the United States since the end of the era of Reconstruction, analyze contemporary factors contributing to the decisions, and consider alternative courses of action.

I.4.HS.2 Evaluate the responses of individuals to historic violations of human dignity involving discrimination, persecution, and crimes against humanity.

I.4.HS.3 Analyze the key decisions by drawing appropriate historical analogies.

I.4.HS.4 Select pivotal decisions in United States history and evaluate them in light of core democratic values and resulting costs and benefits as viewed from a variety of perspectives.

CHAPTER 8

ECONOMICS

When Kuwaiti oil wells were set ablaze during the Gulf War, the price of oil rose because supply was reduced

The Pentagon in Washington, D.C.: military costs are paid for by taxes

A container ship bringing foreign-made goods to the United States

SECTION 1

A CAPSULE SUMMARY OF ECONOMICS

Michigan's High School Test in Social Studies requires you to be familiar with the operation of the U.S. economy. In particular, you should (1) be able to compare our economic system to others; (2) know how our economic system determines what is produced; (3) understand the role government plays in our economy; and (4) appreciate the effects that world trade has. The following summary addresses these topics.

COMPARING OUR ECONOMIC SYSTEM WITH OTHERS

THE THREE BASIC ECONOMIC QUESTIONS

All societies must seek answers to three basic economic questions:

What should be produced?

How should it be produced?

Who should get what is produced?

The method that a society uses to answer these questions is known as its **economic system**. In general, there are three types of economic systems:

Traditional Economy. In a traditional economy, the basic economic questions are answered by tradition. People farm and make things the way their ancestors did. Some families may have special benefits when goods are distributed, simply because their ancestors were privileged in the past. This system provides stability and some measure of security, but at the cost of individual freedom and economic growth.

This farmer uses the same methods his father and grandfather used.

Command Economy. In a command economy, the government answers the basic economic questions. The government decides who makes what and who gets it. Communism in the former Soviet Union (1917-1991) provided an example of a command economy. Many developing nations also adopted command economies in the post-war period, in order to modernize their societies. Command economies have succeeded in accelerating traditional societies into industrial states, but at the cost of sacrificing individual freedom. In the 1970s and 1980s, command economies proved less able to compete with free market economies, which were responsive to consumer needs and allowed a free exchange of information, goods, and services.

Free Market Economy. The free market system is based on individual choice rather than tradition or government command. Individuals invest their own money in businesses to produce and sell goods and services so that they will gain a profit. People are free to produce whatever they wish and to buy whatever they can afford. Government interference in the free market economy is limited. The three basic economic questions are therefore answered by the interplay between **consumers** *(those who buy and use goods and services)* and **producers** *(those who make and sell goods and services)*. The free market system has the following features:

Buyers and sellers interacting in a Central African open-air market

PRIVATE PROPERTY. People have a right to own property and to use it as they see fit.	**FREE ENTERPRISE**. People are free to take part in any business or buy any product. Businesses are free to do anything they wish to attract customers, such as to lower prices or advertise.
PROFIT MOTIVE. The chance of making profits *(what remains after the costs of doing business are paid)* drives people to risk their money in business.	**SUPPLY AND DEMAND**. The forces of supply and demand eliminate less efficient producers and stop the production of unwanted goods. These forces also help to determine the prices of goods sold.

✦ **The Role of Supply and Demand in a Free Market Economy**. Of all the types of economic systems, the free market system seems the most responsive to consumer needs and the best able to stimulate producers. Consumers determine the demand for a product. If a product becomes too expensive, fewer people are willing to buy it. For example, as the graph on page 88 shows, fewer people will buy a pair of shoes costing $100 than if the same shoes cost $10. Through their buying decisions, consumers determine which products will be able to be sold.

Producers determine the *supply*, or availability, of a product. If the price that consumers will pay for a product increases, producers are willing to make more of it.

For example, manufacturers will be willing to invest more money to make more shoes if they can sell them for $100 a pair instead of $25. The interaction between what consumers are willing to pay and what producers are willing to sell determines what is produced. The effects of this interaction are sometimes called the **laws of supply and demand**. Here is how the laws of supply and demand interact in a free market economy:

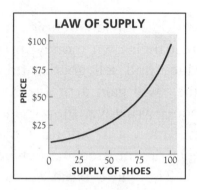

LAW OF SUPPLY

As the price of shoes
goes up, the supply of
shoes increases

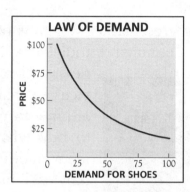

LAW OF DEMAND

As the price of shoes
goes down, the demand
for them increases

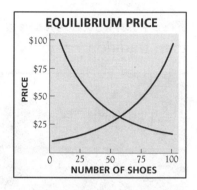

EQUILIBRIUM PRICE

Eventually, the price
reaches an equilibrium
(where the lines intersect)

✦ **How Prices Are Determined in a Market Economy**. If the price is too high, lack of demand will force producers to lower their prices. If the price is too low, consumers will compete for the product, causing producers to raise their prices. Eventually, an equilibrium is reached — at a price that consumers are willing to pay and for which producers are willing to sell.

Mixed Economy. No society has a completely free market economy. In reality, most societies have mixed economic systems in which tradition, government command, and the free market all play a part. The United States primarily has a free market economy, but the government plays an important role in national economic life. You will learn more about the role of government in our economy later in this summary.

This car is being made by a corporation, but is subject to many government regulations.

ECONOMIC GROUPS AND INSTITUTIONS

An **economic group** is a group of people who are involved in some economic activity. The American economy depends on the cooperation of many different economic groups and institutions. Each one produces and consumes goods and services.

MAKING ECONOMIC DECISIONS

Because there are only limited resources to meet unlimited wants, members of each economic group must make decisions about how to earn, spend, and invest their resources. In order to make intelligent decisions, consumers, workers, businesses, and governments must first gather information about any economic question facing them. Gathering different sources is only the beginning in reaching an informed decision. Next, decision-makers must evaluate the information they have obtained by comparing what different sources have to say. Finally, economic decision-makers evaluate the advantages and disadvantages of each option and choose the best one.

Economic decisions are often determined by dollars and cents: taking into account costs and risks, the alternative that promises the most profit or money is usually considered to be the best. But individuals, households, businesses, and government must take into account community values as well as their own profit margins in making economic decisions.

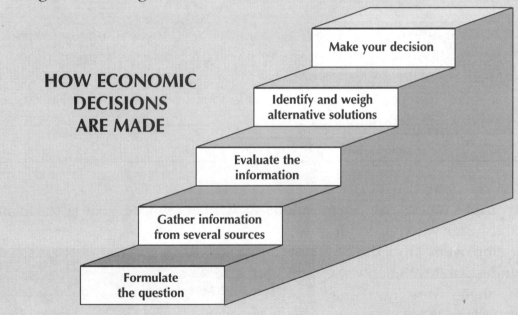

HOW ECONOMIC DECISIONS ARE MADE

- Formulate the question
- Gather information from several sources
- Evaluate the information
- Identify and weigh alternative solutions
- Make your decision

Households. Households perform a dual function in an economy. They act as both consumers and producers. Household members make decisions about where to live, what to eat or wear, and what other things to buy. They also decide how and where to work.

When household members shop, they act as consumers.

HOUSEHOLD DECISION-MAKING

As consumers, household members make daily decisions about what to purchase. Consumers often rely on the experiences of friends or the "brand" name of a product in making such purchases. Various state and federal laws also protect consumers from deception by sellers. One good source of information about consumer products is *Consumer Reports*, a monthly magazine that contains impartial comparisons of products, product recommendations, and reports of product reliability. Consumers also consider the price and availability of goods and services when they shop. Often consumers use **comparison shopping** — shopping for a product in several stores to see where it can be purchased at the best price.

The purchases that the members of a household make form part of a larger strategy in which household members earn, spend, save, and invest. Often, household members will plan a **budget** to ensure they do not buy more things than they can afford. If they make purchases on credit, they must make sure they can pay off the money borrowed over a period of time.

A household budget must also take into account the need to save money for future emergencies and long-term expenses, like paying for college, retirement, or the down payment for a house. To meet these large expenses, many Americans **invest** some of their earnings. Typical investments include stocks, mutual funds, bonds, and certificates of deposit from a bank.

Labor Unions. Labor unions are organizations of workers whose goal is to obtain higher wages and better working conditions from their employers. From the beginning of the Industrial Revolution until the late 1800s, there were no labor unions. Workers toiled for long hours in unsafe conditions. Then workers found that by acting together in a labor union, they had greater influence on their employer. As members of a labor union, workers may engage in **collective bargaining** with their employer, or decide to **strike** (*refuse to work*) until their demands are met.

These airline workers are on strike for higher wages and better working conditions.

Business Firms. A business is a unit of production. Small businesses are usually owned by a single individual, a family, or a small group of people. Small business owners usually run their own businesses on a day-to-day basis. Larger businesses are often **corporations**. People form a corporation by investing money in a company. In exchange, they are given stock, which represents a share in the ownership of the company. A large corporation may have thousands of shareholders.

BUSINESS DECISION-MAKING

The aim of a business is to make a **profit**. A business must carefully examine each opportunity to determine if it will be profitable. Typically, a business considers the costs of providing a particular good or service. This involves calculating each production cost: raw materials, labor, machinery, space to operate in, etc. The business needs to determine if it has enough money or can borrow enough money to cover those costs. Next, the business must determine if it has a market for the product or service it plans to provide, how it will distribute the product, and what consumers will be willing to pay for it. The business also has to take into account whether other producers are offering the same good or service, and what they charge. If the business can keep costs lower than what it receives for selling the product, it will make a profit. Otherwise, it will have a loss and eventually go out of business.

Banks. Banks are special businesses that hold and protect other people's money. People deposit their money in a bank, in checking or savings accounts. Banks pay depositors interest on their savings accounts, and lend the deposited money to other people or businesses. For providing this service, banks charge the borrowers **interest**.

THE ROLE OF GOVERNMENT IN A FREE MARKET ECONOMY

The role of government in our economic life has dramatically changed over the past century. At one time, most Americans believed in **laissez-faire capitalism**. They felt that the government should not interfere in the economy, except to regulate foreign goods and as a referee to ensure fair competition. During the Great Depression of the 1930s, the federal government assumed a much more active role in the economy. Congress passed the **Full Employment Act** in 1946, which set new goals for national economic policy.

During the Great Depression the federal government became the employer of last resort.

Today, the federal government has the principal responsibility to:

<table>
<tr><td>Promote
maximum
employment</td><td>Promote
maximum
production</td><td>Limit
inflation
(rising prices)</td></tr>
</table>

Instruments of Government Economic Policy. To achieve these goals, the federal government has several instruments at its disposal:

✦ **The Power to Provide Public Goods**. Governments can provide goods and services such as military defense and public education directly. Such products are known as **public goods and services**. Sometimes, such as during the New Deal, the government uses its power to provide public goods and services in order to increase employment.

Schools are one of many public goods and services provided by government.

✦ **The Power to Regulate Economic Activities**. The government takes steps to make sure that the marketplace is fair and competitive. It acts as a watchdog over banks, the stock market, and other businesses. Government protects workers, consumers, and the environment by establishing health and safety standards, and ensuring equal opportunity. It also regulates trade by imposing tariffs.

✦ **Taxing Power**. Federal, state, and local governments raise most of the money they need to pay for public goods and services through **taxes** (*money people pay to government*). Governments also can borrow money to pay for their spending. Often, governments issue **bonds**, which pay a fixed interest rate to investors who buy them. This borrowing in turn leads to an increase in the **public debt** — the total amount owed by government.

✦ **Fiscal Policy**. The government influences the economy by its spending, taxing, and borrowing policies. In a **depression** (*severe economic downturn*) the government spends more. By hiring more workers and buying more products, the government creates new jobs. Workers and businesses spend more, increasing demand and stimulating production. But if there is a high rate of inflation, the government slows down the economy by raising taxes. By collecting more money in taxes than it spends, the government encourages producers to lower their prices.

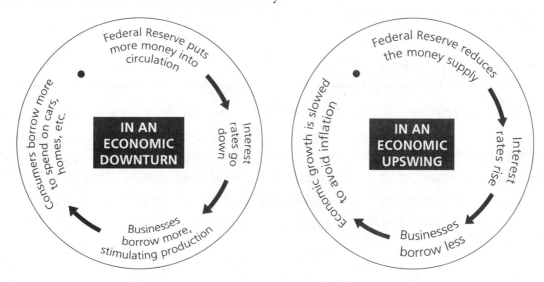

IN AN ECONOMIC DEPRESSION

Government should spend more than it receives in taxes → Government hires more workers, buys more goods → More people are employed; they buy more goods → Consumer demand creates more production & jobs

IN AN INFLATIONARY PERIOD

Government should spend less than it receives in taxes → Consumers will spend less → Businesses spend and borrow less → Reduced consumer demand leads to lower prices

✦ **Monetary Policy**. Another tool the government uses to stabilize the economy is monetary policy. This tool relies on the government's ability to control the total money supply in our economy. The availability of money, in turn, affects the overall amount of business activity. The **Federal Reserve Bank**, an agency of the federal government, controls the ability of banks to lend money. In a depression or recession, the Federal Reserve makes more money available so that interest rates fall. Consumers and businesses borrow more money and make more purchases. When the economy is expanding too fast and prices are rising, the Federal Reserve often raises interest rates and reduces the money supply. This action works to slow down the economy.

IN AN ECONOMIC DOWNTURN

Federal Reserve puts more money into circulation → Interest rates go down → Businesses borrow more, stimulating production → Consumers borrow more to spend on cars, homes, etc.

IN AN ECONOMIC UPSWING

Federal Reserve reduces the money supply → Interest rates rise → Businesses borrow less → Economic growth is slowed to avoid inflation

MEASURING THE NATION'S ECONOMIC HEALTH

To measure the health of our national economy, and to compare it with the economies of other nations, economists look at different statistical indicators. These indicators also influence government leaders in determining our national economic policy:

✦ **Gross Domestic Product (GDP).** This is the value in dollars of all the goods and services produced in a country like the United States in a single year. Sometimes the GDP is referred to as the Gross National Product or GNP.

✦ **Per Capita Income.** This is the Gross Domestic Product divided by the population. It gives us an indication of the average production (or income) of a single person.

✦ **Unemployment Rate.** This measures the number of unemployed people — those who would like to work and are actively looking, but cannot find work.

✦ **National Debt.** This is the total amount of money owed by the government to those who have lent it money by buying government bonds.

Even Halloween pumpkin sales are counted as part of our nation's GDP.

✦ **Inflation Rate.** This measures how quickly prices are increasing for the same goods. When everything seems to cost more than a few years ago, this is a sign of inflation. The **Consumer Price Index** (CPI), based on the average price of a number of typical goods, is often used to keep track of the average prices of consumer goods.

INTERNATIONAL TRADE

The American economy is greatly affected by the world economy and international trade. Increased contact has made nations more interdependent than ever before. Nations are **interdependent** when they depend on trade with one another for goods and services. For example, many American jobs now depend on selling exports. **Exports** are goods and services sold from the United States to other countries. The United States also depends on imports. **Imports** are products from other countries brought into the United States for sale.

The Development of International Trade. All human societies seem to benefit from the voluntary exchange of goods and services. As societies have became more complex, the work of their individual members has become increasingly specialized. Economists refer to this as the **division of labor**. Such specialization depends upon the exchange of goods and services that the individual members of a society produce.

Increasing specialization has also encouraged the growth of international trade. Since earliest times, prehistoric peoples have been known to have traded goods with their neighbors. In the ancient world, trade was based on the exchange of valuable products like pottery, olive oil, textiles, and precious metals. At first, these goods were simply exchanged by **barter**. Eventually, copper, gold, silver became the **medium of exchange**. Monarchs stamped pieces of gold and silver of uniform size and weight to create the first coinage. Merchants from different countries traded goods for these coins.

Because of a strong U.S. economy, American dollars are welcomed throughout the world.

In the 1700s, countries began printing paper currency. Governments promised to pay the holders of these paper notes with gold or silver. When one country held too much paper currency from another country, it would simply redeem this currency in gold. Today, international trade is based on the promises of individual governments to support their currencies, but is no longer tied to the gold standard.

Why Nations Trade. Most nations do not produce everything they need. As a result, nations trade with other nations to obtain many products. Because countries have different locations, climates, and natural resources, some nations can produce certain goods at a lower cost or more efficiently than other nations. The soil and climate of Colombia, for example, give it an advantage over the United States in growing coffee beans.

A tanker brings Middle Eastern oil to the United States.

In general, nations are better off specializing — putting their money, resources, and labor into making those things at which they are most efficient in producing. Each country is generally better off trading those products it makes best and using the money it gets to buy other goods and services from other nations. Economists refer to this as the theory of **comparative advantage**. All countries benefit as a result.

BUSINESS DECISION-MAKING: GOING INTERNATIONAL

One decision many successful U.S. businesses must make is whether to go international by exporting their products abroad. In addition to the cost of producing and distributing their goods or services in the United States, these businesses must take into consideration certain other factors that relate to selling or operating in foreign countries:

- the costs of shipping the product and any tariff duties they will have to pay or quotas that may be imposed on them;
- any fees that need to be paid to foreign agents and distributors;
- the need to comply with the rules and product standards of the foreign country;
- the expense of changing foreign currency into U.S. dollars; and
- the special problems and risks of operating abroad, such as the risk of political instability in the foreign country.

These businesses must also consider whether foreign consumers will have the same demand for their product as American consumers, or whether foreign products or substitutes will have a competitive edge. If, after weighing all of these factors, an American business still thinks it can make a substantial profit overseas, it will probably try to export its goods and services.

The Effects of Global Interdependence. Global interdependence, economic specialization, and economic development are closely related. Countries develop more rapidly when they are able to produce goods and services in demand on world markets. Economic interdependence also encourages **cultural diffusion** — the exchange of ideas, technology, and culture that accompanies the exchange of goods.

Trade. Americans depend on oil bought from other countries, and their ability to sell items like computers and medicines abroad.

Technology. The Chinese depend on new manufacturing technology provided by European and U.S. investors.

Resources. Japan depends on oil it purchases from the Mideast to power its factories and automobiles.

THE MANY FACES OF GLOBAL INTERDEPENDENCE

Investment. Latin American nations depend on capital investments from the United States and Europe.

Environment. Canadians depend on Americans to enforce anti-pollution laws to reduce the acid rain falling on their forests.

Defense. The member countries of NATO depend on each other for defense against attacks.

THE SPECIAL PROBLEMS OF DEVELOPING NATIONS

One way to understand a nation's economy is to compare its various economic indicators with those of other nations.

Comparing the U.S. with Some Developing Nations. Countries with high production and high per capita incomes are often called **developed nations**. Nations that are trying to make more effective use of their resources are called **developing nations**.

SELECTED DEVELOPED AND DEVELOPING NATIONS

	United States (No. America)	Zaire (Africa)	Haiti (Latin America)	Bangladesh (South Asia)	Yemen (Middle East)
Total Population	265 million	46.5 million	6.7 million	123 million	13 million
Per Capita Income ($ US)	$27,607	$440	$870	$1,040	$1,955
Automobiles	146,000,000	94,000	32,000	75,000	186,000
Telephones	1 per 1.7 people	1 per 1,140 people	1 per 164 people	1 per 435 people	1 per 83 people
Life Expectancy (in years)	73 (male) 79 (female)	45 (male) 49 (female)	47 (male) 51 (female)	56 (male) 56 (female)	58 (male) 61 (female)
Number of Doctors	1 per 391 people	1 per 15,586 people	1 per 10,060 people	1 per 5,264 people	1 per 3,900 people
Literacy Rate	96%	77%	45%	38%	39%
Imports/ Exports	$749 billion/ $685 billion	$356 million/ $362 million	$477 million/ $173 million	$4 billion/ $2.4 billion	$2.6 billion/ $1.75 billion

Developing countries often face some special economic problems:

Unskilled Workforce. Developing nations often lack a skilled workforce. A majority of the population are peasant farmers who work by hand.

Need for Capital Investment. Developing countries usually need roads and bridges, better communications systems, and newer manufacturing facilities.

PROBLEMS FACING DEVELOPING NATIONS

Foreign Competition. Developing countries often cannot make goods cheaply enough because they lack skilled workers, technology, and capital investment.

Population Growth. Birth rates are often high in developing nations, outpacing economic growth.

STRATEGIES GOVERNMENTS USE TO OVERCOME THESE PROBLEMS

In developing countries, the government often plays a special role in dealing with economic problems and promoting economic growth.

✦ **Command Economies**. In the post-World War II period, many developing countries adopted Communism or other forms of central planning to promote more rapid economic development. These governments encouraged the development and introduction of heavy industry and modern technology. Ultimately, they proved unresponsive to local and global economic needs.

COMMUNISM

Communism developed in 19th-century Europe from the ideas of Karl Marx. Communists believed that factory owners and other capitalists exploited their workers. Communists predicted that workers eventually would rebel, and establish a "classless" society. Russia became the first Communist country in 1917, when the Bolshevik Party took over the entire economy and government. Communist leaders formulated national five-year plans, deciding what state-owned factories would produce. Emphasis was placed on heavy industry and a powerful military. In agriculture, the government took away farmers' lands and formed "collective" farms where people were paid wages and forced to produce food for the state.

Eventually, Communist systems could not keep up with the free market economies of the West. People in Communist countries had little incentive to work hard, because they received the same wages without regard to how much they produced. Information was not freely communicated, and the government's central planners failed to predict many of the economic needs of society. In practice, Communist societies could not provide equality, freedom, or an efficient market to their citizens.

✦ **Green Revolution**. In the 1960s and 1970s, many developing countries improved food production by applying modern technology. New fertilizers, pesticides, and irrigation were introduced, and special seeds produced bumper crops.

✦ **Population Control**. Some developing nations introduced programs to reduce their high birth rates. They developed family planning centers and taught new birth control methods. China introduced its "one-child" policy.

✦ **Free-Market Approach**. In the late 1980s and 1990s, many nations turned to the free-market system to improve their economies. They developed exports to earn more money for domestic investment. Foreign investors were attracted to developing countries because labor costs were low. Encouraging exports still appears to be the best strategy for promoting the economic growth of developing nations.

SECTION 2

MAJOR ECONOMIC TERMS AND CONCEPTS

Use this graphic organizer to review your understanding of important economics terms and concepts.

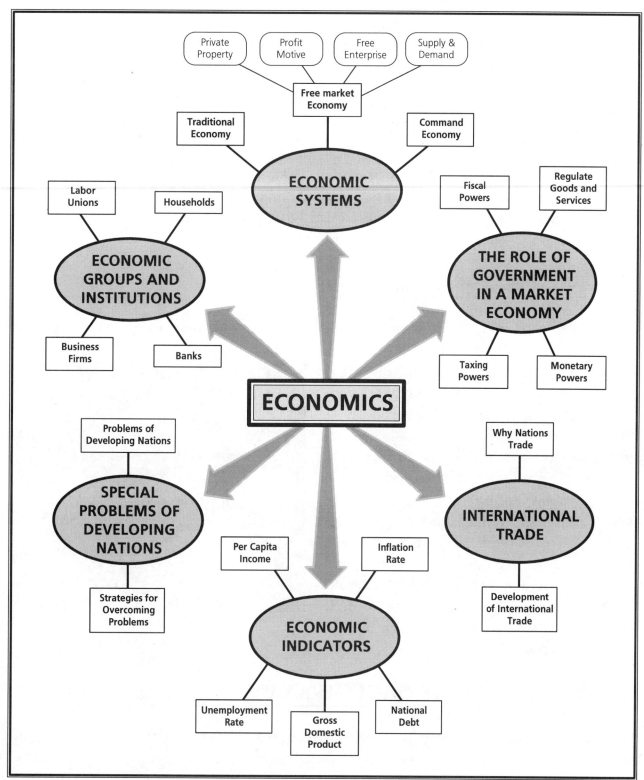

Prompts are used to test your understanding of the main ideas and facts of social studies. This section summarizes Michigan's content standards for economics.

STANDARD IV.1: INDIVIDUAL AND HOUSEHOLD CHOICES

This standard looks at how individuals and households make economic decisions in a free market economy. You should be able to design a strategy for earning, spending, saving, and investing the resources of a typical American household. You should also be able to analyze the ways individuals select suppliers of goods and services and protect themselves from deception in the marketplace.

STANDARD IV.2: BUSINESS CHOICES

This standard examines how businesses make choices in organizing, producing, and using resources. You should be able to outline the decision-making process a business might go through in deciding whether to export to a foreign market. For example, it would have to evaluate costs, risks, and potential profits. Would there be foreign markets for its product? What customs duties and legal requirements would it face? How would it be affected by receiving foreign currency? You should also be able to evaluate ways to resolve conflicts between business interests and community values. For example, should a business be able to build a factory in a residential area, or dismiss excess employees?

A woman exchanges dollars for foreign currency. Do businesses need to be concerned with this?

STANDARD IV.3: ROLE OF GOVERNMENT

This standard focuses on how government decisions affect the economy — especially decisions on taxation, public spending, public goods, and regulation. You should be able to distinguish between monetary and fiscal policy, and explain how each of these might be applied to problems like unemployment or inflation. You should be able to identify different indicators governments use to measure the functioning of their economies, such as Gross Domestic Product, inflation, and the unemployment rate. You should be able to compare different approaches used by various governments in developing countries to promote economic growth, such as state-owned enterprises and encouraging exports. Finally, you should be able to evaluate a government spending program by looking at its intended and unintended results.

STANDARD IV.4: ECONOMIC SYSTEMS

This standard focuses on how economic systems work. You should know how producers and consumers interact in a free market economy to determine what is produced and the prices at which items are sold. You should be able to describe the relationship between our domestic economy and the international economic system. You should be able to compare the free market system of the United States with other free market systems as well as with traditional and command economies around the world, and to evaluate these different systems based on how well they deliver efficiency, equality, freedom, stability, security, and economic growth. Finally, you should be able to identify the various economic institutions within these systems, including households, business firms, banks, government agencies, and labor unions, and describe their relationships.

STANDARD IV.5: TRADE

This standard focuses on the importance of trade. You should be able to compare the benefits and problems of an economic system based on the voluntary exchange of goods and services — that is, a free market system. You should also be able to trace the historical development of international trading ties. For example, ancient peoples traded with one another and passed on ideas and technology as well as exchanging goods and services. You should also be able to explain how international economic specialization, global economic interdependence, and economic development are related. Finally, you should be able to describe the

A McDonald's in Helsinki, Finland — one small example of our interdependent global economy

effects of currency exchange, tariffs, quotas, and product standards on both world trade and domestic economic activities.

SECTION 4

PRACTICE QUESTIONS

This section contains practice questions about economics. There are two clusters of selected-response questions. Examine each prompt carefully and answer the five questions that follow it. There are also two constructed-response questions, each with a prompt and a writing task. After examining the prompt carefully, write your answers as directed. Each question has the benchmark number of the content standard being tested. A list of economics benchmarks is at the end of this chapter.

— SELECTED-RESPONSE QUESTIONS —

Directions: Read the following passage and use it with what you already know to answer the questions that follow:

GOVERNMENT SPENDING AND THE SUPERFUND

The residents of Pitman, New Jersey, knew something was wrong when pink, foamy water began oozing up in their yards. Soon afterward, they learned that Pitman's cancer rate was much higher than the national average. An investigation by the Environmental Protection Agency (EPA) found that Pitman was built near a landfill that contained 46,000 barrels of cancer-causing chemicals. Over 90,000 tons of contaminated soil was dug up and trucked to a purification plant. The cost of this operation was $100 million.

Who is responsible for protecting the environment?

Who paid for this? In 1980, Congress created the Superfund to identify toxic-waste sites, find the companies responsible for them, and make the polluters pay for part of the cleanup. According to EPA figures, of 38,000 hazardous-waste sites, the Superfund has cleaned up only 150. Yet the Superfund has cost taxpayers $22 billion, much of which has been spent on legal costs in contests with accused polluters rather than in actually cleaning up sites.

Critics argue the Superfund has been a "super failure." They urge the EPA to be more realistic about the way it spends its limited resources. Containing many of the contaminants, they believe, would often be less expensive and more effective than cleaning them up, and would reduce legal costs.

1 Which statement represents a conclusion that might be drawn from the passage?

   A Only Federal agencies should handle environmental issues.

   B Economic indicators often predict economic problems before they become fully evident.

   C Government programs can have unintended as well as intended results.

   D Consumers must learn to protect themselves from deception in the marketplace.

   IV.3.HS.4

2 Which core democratic value was reflected in the decision to create the Superfund?

   A the common good

   B equality

   C checks and balances

   D individual rights

   IV.4.HS.3

3 Critics of the way the Superfund has been administered would most likely refer to the economic concept of

   A comparative advantage

   B division of labor

   C supply and demand

   D opportunity cost

   IV.4.HS.3

4 The reading passage describes a conflict between

   A private business interests and community values

   B consumer spending and saving

   C local and national priorities

   D fiscal and monetary policy

   IV.2.HS.2

5 Which regulatory power of the federal government is described in this passage?

   A the power to encourage competition in the marketplace

   B the power to protect workers and consumers

   C the power to promote international trade

   D the power to ensure equal opportunity

   IV.4.HS.3

Name _____ Teacher _____

Directions: Study the following passage and graphs and use them with what you already know to answer the questions that follow.

JOHN'S QUICK BURGER SHOP

John's new restaurant will officially open next week. Based upon the experiences of other fast-food restaurants in the area, the **first** graph shows the number of hamburgers that John is likely to sell to customers at various prices. The **second** graph indicates how many hamburgers John would be willing to sell at different prices.

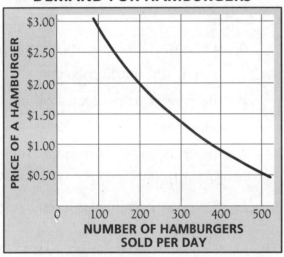

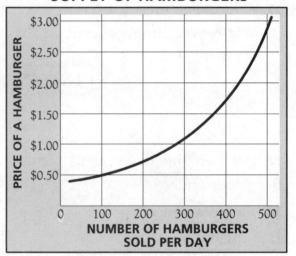

6 The relationship between the supply of and demand for hamburgers shown in the graphs illustrates which idea?

A Opportunity costs determine prices.

B A voluntary exchange of goods is used in a barter system.

C Prices are determined by the interaction of supply and demand in a free market economy.

D Government regulations have an impact on fast-food restaurants.

IV.4.HS.1

7 In a free market economy, what would be the MOST likely selling price for a hamburger at John's restaurant?

A About $3.00

B About $2.00

C About $1.25

D About 50¢

IV.4.HS.1

8 What would PROBABLY happen to John's business if the amount of beef available suddenly decreased?

A The price of John's hamburgers would increase.

B The supply of hamburgers to John's restaurant would increase.

C The price of John's hamburgers would decrease.

D The price of John's hamburgers would remain unchanged.

IV.4.HS.1

9 What conclusion can be drawn from John's new business venture?

A The per capita income in the United States is the highest in the world.

B The United States has a free market economy.

C The United States is the leading economic power in the world.

D The United States imports most of its beef.

IV.4.HS.5

10 Which of the following would probably lead to an increase in the demand for John's hamburgers?

A An increase in the price of John's hamburgers

B A decrease in the incomes of John's potential customers

C An increase in the profits of John's restaurant

D An increase in the price of fried chicken, pizza, and hot dogs in other local fast-food restaurants

IV.3.HS.1

Name _____ Teacher _____

106

— CONSTRUCTED-RESPONSE QUESTIONS —

Directions: You should take about 5 minutes to read the following material and use it with what you already know to complete this task.

TO SELL OR NOT TO SELL

Matt and Susan are the owners of the XYZ Bicycle Company — the nation's leading bicycle manufacturer. An Asian country has just announced that it is ending its import restrictions on American goods. Matt and Susan are interested in increasing their bicycle sales, and are now considering whether to export to this country. Before making their decision, here are some factors that Matt and Susan should take into account:

- shipping costs to Asia are on the rise
- U.S bicycle sales have been stable for the last five years
- this Asian nation has one of the world's largest populations
- XYZ Bicycle Company's factory is operating at 90% of capacity
- new machines to increase manufacturing capacity are very expensive
- interest rates for business loans from banks are at an all-time high

11 On the lines provided, make and explain your decision regarding whether or not Matt and Susan should sell bicycles to this Asian nation.

Your decision about selling bicycles to this Asian nation: _____

Explanation of your decision, referring to two of the factors listed above: _____

_____

_____

_____

_____

_____

_____

_____

_____

_____

IV.2.HS.2

Name _____ Teacher _____

Directions: You should take about 5 minutes to study the following illustration and use it with what you already know to complete this task.

ECONOMIC INDICATORS

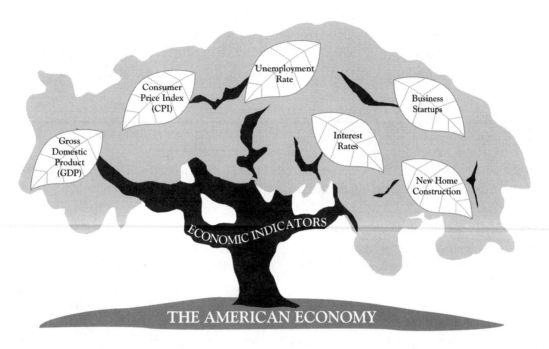

12 On the lines provided, select **two** indicators from the illustration and describe how each one is used to measure the state of the American economy.

Identification of indicator: _____

Description of how it is used to measure the state of our economy:_____

_____

_____

Identification of indicator: _____

Description of how it is used to measure the state of our economy: _____

_____

_____

IV.3.HS.1

Name _____ Teacher _____

BENCHMARKS OF THE ECONOMICS STRAND

Standard IV.1: Individual and Household Choices

IV.1.HS.1 Design a strategy for earning, spending, saving, and investing resources.

IV.1.HS.2 Evaluate the impact on households of alternative solutions to societal problems such as healthcare, housing, or energy use.

IV.1.HS.3 Analyze ways individuals can select suppliers of goods and services and protect themselves from deception in the marketplace.

Standard IV.2: Business Choices

IV.2.HS.1 Outline a decision-making process a business might go through when deciding whether to export to a foreign market.

IV.2.HS.2 Evaluate ways to resolve conflicts resulting from differences between business interests and community values.

Standard IV.3: Role of Government

IV.3.HS.1 Describe the use of economic indicators and assess their accuracy.

IV.3.HS.2 Distinguish between monetary and fiscal policy and explain how each might be applied to problems such as unemployment and inflation.

IV.3.HS.3 Compare governmental approaches to economic growth in developing countries.

IV.3.HS.4 Evaluate a government spending program on the basis of its intended and unintended results.

Standard IV.4: Economic Systems

IV.4.HS.1 Use case studies to exemplify how supply and demand, prices, incentives, and profits determine what is produced and distributed in a competitive world market.

IV.4.HS.2 Describe relationships between a domestic economy and the international economic system.

IV.4.HS.3 Evaluate the United States and other economic systems on their ability to achieve broad social goals such as freedom, efficiency, equity, security, development, and stability.

IV.4.HS.4 Describe relationships among the various economic institutions that comprise economic systems such as households, business firms, banks, government agencies, and labor unions.

IV.4.HS.5 Compare and contrast a free market economic system with other economic systems.

Standard IV.5: Trade

IV.5.HS.1 Evaluate the benefits and problems of an economic system built on voluntary exchange.

IV.5.HS.2 Trace the historical development of international trading ties.

IV.5.HS.3 Explain how specialization, interdependence, and economic development are related.

IV.5.HS.4 Describe the effect of currency exchange, tariffs, quotas, and product standards on world trade and domestic economic activity.

CHAPTER 9

CIVICS

John F. Kennedy campaigning for President, 1960

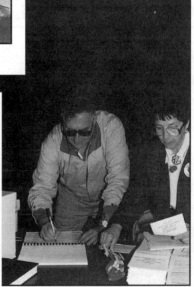

A citizen votes in an election

Pledging allegiance to the flag

SECTION 1: A Capsule Summary of Civics

SECTION 2: Major Civics Terms and Concepts

SECTION 3: The Content Standards for Civics

SECTION 4: Practice Questions

A CAPSULE SUMMARY OF CIVICS

Michigan's High School Test in Social Studies requires you to be familiar with the constitutional foundations of American government. You should know: (1) the ideals of the Declaration of Independence and how they have helped citizens deal with the challenges of diversity; (2) the basic principles of American government; (3) how Americans apply abstract democratic principles to concrete situations; (4) how the branches of our government check one another, including how the U.S. Supreme Court strikes down unconstitutional laws; and (5) America's role in world affairs. The following summary addresses each of these topics.

THE IDEALS OF THE DECLARATION OF INDEPENDENCE

Unlike the countries of Europe of the time, the United States adopted a democratic form of government when it became independent. The principal beliefs of those who created our government were best expressed in the Declaration of Independence.

What Is Government? People are social beings: they need to live with others in groups or communities. As a result, communities need to make rules to settle disagreements among their members and to protect the community from those who violate its rules. The organization set up to protect the community is called **government**. Just as a pilot guides a ship, a government guides the members of a community in their dealings with themselves and outsiders. All governments are given powers to carry out their authority over the members of society. These powers include:

> **a *legislative* power to make laws**

> **an *executive* power to carry out laws**

> **a *judicial* power to interpret laws**

The Meaning of the Declaration of Independence. In 1776, after the outbreak of the American Revolutionary War, American colonists sent representatives to a "Continental Congress" in Philadelphia. The members of the Continental Congress quickly decided to break away from Great Britain. Thomas Jefferson and others formed a special committee to write a Declaration of Independence to explain to the world why the colonists decided to seek independence. The Declaration was issued by the Continental Congress on **July 4, 1776**.

The first paragraph of the Declaration gave a general explanation of why governments exist. It stated that all men are created equal and that governments should protect the rights of individual citizens. The language of the Declaration implied that all citizens should enjoy equal rights, even though its authors did not themselves extend equal rights to women, slaves, or those without property.

The Declaration continued with a list of grievances which the American colonists had suffered from the British government, thus justifying the colonists' demand for independence. The Declaration of Independence is considered one of the most important documents in American history, and established a firm foundation for individual liberty in the United States.

We hold these truths to be self-evident, that all men are created equal ... they are endowed by their Creator with certain unalienable Rights, [and] among these are Life, Liberty and the pursuit of Happiness. [T]o secure these rights, Governments are instituted among Men, deriving their just powers from the consent of the governed ... whenever any Form of Government becomes destructive of these ends, it is the right of the People to alter or abolish it, and to institute new Government ...

Birth of the United States. With the Declaration, the American colonies became independent of Great Britain.

Foundation for Democratic Government. The U.S. would have a democratic government in which final power was held by citizens.

SIGNIFICANCE OF THE DECLARATION OF INDEPENDENCE

Inspiration for Equality. The Declaration's ideal of human equality set a goal for the U.S. that is gradually being met 200 years later.

Influence on the Constitution. Many rights guaranteed in the U.S. Constitution were based on ideas set forth in the Declaration.

Impact Abroad. The Declaration's powerful logic influenced people in Asia, Africa, Latin America and the Middle East to fight for their rights.

PRINCIPLES OF THE U.S. CONSTITUTION

Government authority is a matter of great concern to each of us. Why do we give people whom we hardly know such power over our lives? And how much power can we give to our government without allowing it to threaten our liberties? These questions help us to appreciate the difficulties that faced the framers of our system of government who met in Philadelphia at the Constitutional Convention of 1787.

To create a balanced system of government that would provide order without threatening individual liberties, the members of the Constitutional Convention adopted the following principles:

Popular Sovereignty. Their most basic principle was **popular sovereignty** — that the people themselves should decide what they want by majority rule. This principle is stated in the **Preamble** (*introduction*) to the U.S. Constitution. Its opening words, "We the People ...," tells us that the right to form a government rested with the citizens themselves. The Constitution further established a government of elected officials in order to keep supreme political power with the people. Laws are made by our elected representatives in Congress, and enforced by elected officials like the President. The rest of the Preamble identifies what its authors believed should be the goals of our national government.

> We, the People of the United States,
> - in order to form a more perfect Union,
> - establish justice,
> - ensure domestic tranquillity,
> - provide for the common defense,
> - promote the general welfare,
> - and secure the blessings of liberty to ourselves and our posterity,
>
> do ordain and establish this Constitution for the United States of America.

This system of democratic government differs from other forms of government like **dictatorship**, in which one individual or a small group holds supreme political power, or a **monarchy**, in which a ruler holds power through inherited right.

Federalism. The writers of the Constitution feared giving too much power to the central government. Instead, they wanted to balance power between the national government and the thirteen state governments. To do this, they introduced **federalism,** a system of government in which political power is shared. Our national *(federal)* government deals with matters that affect the whole country, while state governments mainly handle affairs relating to each individual state.

This federal system has the advantage of allowing citizens a greater voice in matters that affect them closely without affecting citizens in other states. However, federalism sometimes makes it difficult to set national standards in such fields as education or civil rights. In order to achieve national uniformity in some matters, our national government often exercises its power to control interstate commerce *(trade between states)* and things that affect interstate commerce.

U.S. soldiers train at Fort Bragg. Control of our armed forces is a task assigned to the federal government.

Limited Government. The authors of the Constitution took great care to *limit* government power by spelling out the specific powers of the federal government. The federal government can only use those powers which are given to it in the Constitution itself. These are known as **delegated powers**. For example, the U. S. Congress has the power to coin money. Other government powers are reserved for the states. However, one important clause, sometimes known as the **elastic clause,** allows Congress to expand or stretch its powers in some situations. This clause gives Congress the power to enact any laws that it deems "necessary and proper" for accomplishing its delegated powers.

Supremacy of the National Government. The framers of the Constitution realized that there were bound to be future conflicts between the federal government and the state governments. Anticipating such conflicts, they added the **Supremacy Clause**. This clause states that valid federal laws, so long as they are constitutional, are superior to conflicting state laws.

Separation of Powers. The authors of the Constitution feared concentrating too much power in the federal government, since they had just recently been oppressed by British power. Therefore, they **separated** the three main powers of government into different branches — **legislative**, **executive**, and **judicial**. They believed this separation would make it difficult for any one person or branch of government to become too powerful. State governments, such as the government of Michigan, follow a similar pattern of separating powers among three branches.

SEPARATION OF POWERS

LEGISLATIVE BRANCH Power to make the laws	**EXECUTIVE BRANCH** Power to carryout the laws	**JUDICIAL BRANCH** Power to interpret the laws

	LEGISLATIVE POWER	**EXECUTIVE POWER**	**JUDICIAL POWER**
NATIONAL GOVERNMENT	Congress	President	Supreme Court
STATE OF NEW YORK	State Legislature	Governor	Court of Appeals
STATE OF MICHIGAN	State Legislature	Governor	Supreme Court

As part of our system of separation of powers, the authors of the Constitution created a separately elected President. This differs from the Parliamentary system of government in countries like Great Britain:

♦ **Parliamentary Government**. Voters elect the legislature, called **Parliament**, whose members then choose the chief executive, known as the **Prime Minister**, from among their own members. The Prime Minister is in charge of both leading Parliament and enforcing the laws.

♦ **Presidential Government**. Voters separately elect both the legislature and the President. The President and his Cabinet are never members of the legislative branch. Both the executive and the legislative branches are therefore independent branches and co-equal to each other.

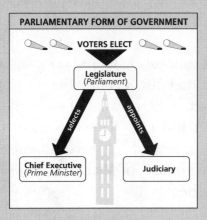

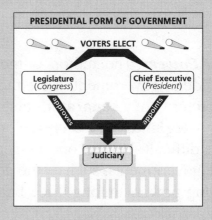

How Checks and Balances Work. To further ensure that no branch of the federal government became too powerful, the Constitution gave each branch ways to "check" (*limit*) the other branches. For example, the Senate must approve most Presidential appointments. On the other hand, the President can **veto** (*refuse to sign*) laws that Congress passes. Congress can override a veto, but only if two-thirds of the House and Senate vote in favor of the override. Power was thus "balanced" among the branches so that important decisions could not be made without a general agreement.

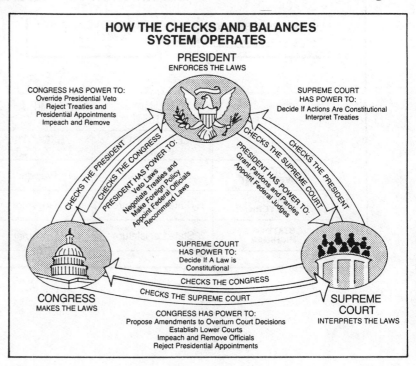

Flexibility. Although written over 200 years ago, the Constitution has proven flexible enough to keep up with the changing needs of our country. Changing interpretations of the Constitution by the U.S. Supreme Court help adapt the Constitution to new conditions. The Constitution also keeps pace through the process of amendment (*addition*). It is more difficult to amend the Constitution, however, than to pass an ordinary law. Three quarters of the states must agree to an amendment for it to be approved.

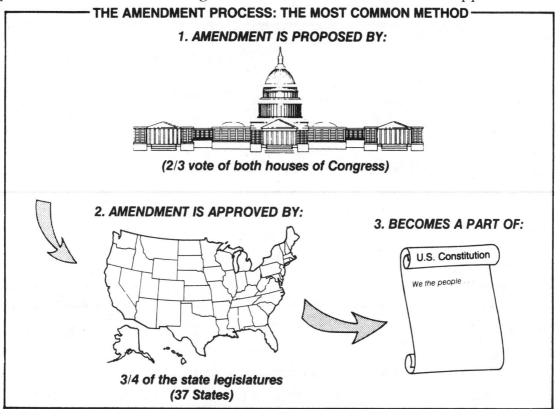

THE AMENDMENT PROCESS: THE MOST COMMON METHOD

1. AMENDMENT IS PROPOSED BY:

(2/3 vote of both houses of Congress)

2. AMENDMENT IS APPROVED BY:

3. BECOMES A PART OF:

U.S. Constitution

We the people . . .

3/4 of the state legislatures
(37 States)

INDIVIDUAL RIGHTS

When the Constitution was first written, it contained no guarantee of individual liberties. The Bill of Rights, proposed by the first Congress, was added to the Constitution in the form of the first ten amendments. A second milestone in the protection of individual liberties was the passage of the Fourteenth Amendment.

The First Amendment. The First Amendment guarantees that Congress cannot pass a law taking away the freedom of religion, free speech, freedom of the press, freedom to assemble, or the freedom to ask government officials to change the laws. Our First Amendment freedoms are not unlimited. For example, freedom of speech does not mean we can say whatever we want in all circumstances. A person cannot yell "Fire!" in a crowded movie theater as a joke. This would endanger people's lives. But restriction of free speech is justified only if a real threat of present danger exists. For this reason, the Supreme Court denies most attempts by government to limit freedom of speech.

The Rights of the Accused. Our public officials hold the power to search our homes, put us in jail, and, in extreme cases, to take our lives. The Bill of Rights devoted the Fourth, Fifth, Sixth, and Eighth Amendments to prohibiting government officials from taking a person's life, liberty, or property without fair and reasonable legal procedures. Some of these procedures, known as "**due process of law,**" can be identified as follows:

Fourth Amendment: A person's property cannot be searched or taken away without fair and reasonable legal procedures.

Fifth Amendment: People cannot be required to give evidence against themselves. The Supreme Court has also ruled that people in police custody must be informed of their constitutional rights before being questioned.

Sixth Amendment: People accused of a crime have a right to a fair and impartial trial. They must be told of the charges against them. They have the right to a jury, and to be represented by a lawyer.

Eighth Amendment: Courts cannot punish someone in a cruel or unusual way.

Fourteenth Amendment. When it was first passed, the Bill of Rights protected individuals from the actions of the federal government but not from the actions of state governments. After the Civil War, the **Fourteenth Amendment** (1868) was adopted to protect citizens from abuses by state governments. It did this in two ways:

✦ **Due Process Rights.** State governments must follow the same procedures as the federal government when arresting, searching, and convicting persons suspected of a crime. States cannot take away a person's freedom of expression except for the same narrow reasons that the federal government can.

✦ **Equal Protection Rights.** The Fourteenth Amendment also guarantees citizens the "equal protection" of the laws. State governments cannot treat some groups differently from others unless there is a compelling reason. For example, a state government can refuse to allow three-year olds to vote, since it's clear that they are not mature enough. But a state government cannot refuse to let some people vote because of their race or ethnic background.

ACHIEVING AMERICAN IDEALS

The realities of life in the United States have not always lived up to the promise of American ideals, as reflected in such documents as the Declaration of Independence and the U.S. Constitution. For example, despite amendments guaranteeing the right to vote, many African Americans in Southern states were long denied their voting rights.

Beginning in the late 1800s, the leaders of many disadvantaged groups, especially African Americans and women, organized reform movements to improve their conditions and to create an environment that would be free of discrimination.

Suffragists on the march in 1912. Women struggled from 1848 to 1920 to gain the right to vote.

- ✦ **Nineteenth Amendment** (1920). This guaranteed women the right to vote throughout the United States.

- ✦ **Brown v. Board of Education.** In 1954, the Supreme Court ruled that racial segregation (*the separation of blacks and whites*) in public schools was unconstitutional because separate schools were by their nature unequal. The case was an important turning point in ending segregation in schools and other aspects of public life.

Public places in some parts of the U.S. were segregated before the Brown *decision.*

- ✦ **Affirmative Action Programs**. In 1965, President Lyndon B. Johnson signed an order requiring employers with federal contracts to hire minorities and women. These programs increased minority and female representation in colleges, professions, and in many businesses and occupations.

- ✦ **From the Civil Rights Act to the Americans with Disabilities Act**. The Civil Rights Act of 1964 prohibited racial, gender, and religious discrimination in businesses affected by interstate commerce. In 1990, Congress passed an act that guaranteed disabled people would be treated equally in their jobs and would be given easier access to office buildings, stores, restaurants, trains, and buses.

THE RULE OF LAW

Fundamental to the American system of government is the "rule of law." A **law** tells people what they can or cannot do. Usually there is a **penalty** (*punishment*) for breaking the law. Because we have a written set of laws, each of us is subject to the same rules. Government officials cannot fine or imprison us unless we break those rules. This "rule of law" promotes fairness and equality.

118

Law and the Judicial Branch. Courts play a special role in promoting the rule of law. You have often heard that courts "apply" the law, but what does this mean? One function of courts is to find out the facts by examining the evidence. A second function of courts is to "interpret" the law. No general rule can ever be so precise that it can foresee all the possible situations that might arise. For this reason, we need courts to apply laws to specific situations — to see whether a particular circumstance falls within the rule. Suppose, for example, we see the following sign:

It seems clear that this sign means no cars or trucks are permitted in the park, but what about bicycles? Are they banned because they are a danger to pedestrians? What about baby strollers or wheelchairs? Are they also "vehicles" in the sense intended by the sign? To decide the meaning, courts must interpret the words of a law or rule. Sometimes they consider the purpose of the rule, or what was said about it when it was made, to determine whether it applies to a particular situation. A court might say that the purpose of the rule "**NO VEHICLES IN THE PARK**" is to avoid danger to pedestrians. Since wheelchairs and baby strollers pose no danger to pedestrians, they are not "vehicles" in the sense intended by the rule.

Because we live under the "rule of law," we expect everyone to be treated identically by the law. Courts therefore follow the example of other courts unless there is some reason not to do so. The rulings of judges thus provide another source of law in addition to the laws passed by legislatures. This judge-made law is often called the **common law**.

Type of Cases. Courts perform several functions. They apply criminal laws by putting those accused of crimes on trial and sentencing them if they are found guilty. They apply government regulations by fining offenders. They also decide **civil cases** — disputes that may involve family law (*divorce or child custody*), business law (*contract disagreements*), or personal injuries (*disputes over who should pay for accidental injuries*).

In any court proceeding, each party has the right to an attorney, the right to hear the opposing evidence, the right to present one's case, and the right to appeal the decision. In criminal cases and some civil cases, the defendant also has the right to have the case tried by a **jury** — a panel of unbiased citizens. The judge decides what evidence can be admitted into consideration, and instructs the jury on what the legal issues are and exactly what they are to decide. These help ensure that each side gets a fair opportunity to persuade the judge and jury that it is correct.

By applying laws, courts help preserve the social order. Parties may not agree with the result of a court decision, but they generally agree with the procedures used by the court to make its decision. This generally makes an unfavorable decision more acceptable to the losing party.

Unlawful to photocopy

ORGANIZATION OF THE U.S. COURT SYSTEM

The United States has two main levels of courts: state courts and federal courts. There are also local courts, such as municipal courts.

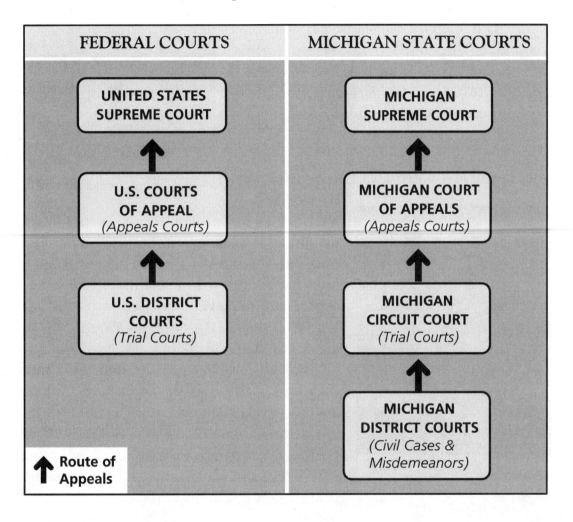

- ✦ **Trial Courts.** These courts generally hear each side present its case, including the examination of witnesses and the submission of evidence. Trial courts at the state level can hear almost any kind of case. Federal district courts, in contrast, are more limited. They can only try cases that involve federal law or citizens from different states.

- ✦ **Appeals Courts**. When a trial court gives its verdict, each party usually has the right to appeal the decision. An appellate court usually is limited to reviewing the issues of law presented by the case. Did the trial court apply the law correctly to the facts presented by the case? If the appellate court decides that the trial court misapplied the law, it can overturn the decision and send the case back to the trial court to be retried.

◆ **The Role of the U.S. Supreme Court.** The Supreme Court operates as our nation's highest "Court of Appeals." It can hear appeals from federal courts and also from the highest state courts when these involve issues of federal law or the U.S. Constitution. The exercise of this power of review is left up to the Court's own discretion. Since they can hear only a few hundred cases each year, the Justices of the Supreme Court usually choose to decide cases of the greatest political and legal significance.

The U.S. Supreme Court Building

The Supreme Court plays two roles. It can determine how an ordinary federal law should be applied to a particular case, as other courts do. The Supreme Court also has a second role that accounts for its great importance in our political life. This role is known as **judicial review** — deciding whether a law itself is constitutional. The Supreme Court can actually reject a law passed by Congress if it believes that the law violates the U.S. Constitution. The only way to override the Court's decision in such a situation is to amend the Constitution, or for a later Supreme Court to overturn the decision. The Supreme Court never decides the constitutionality of a law until after the law is passed and an actual dispute has arisen that is appealed to the Supreme Court.

Chief Justice John Marshall strengthened the Court's power of judicial review

DEMOCRACY IN ACTION: APPLYING DEMOCRATIC PRINCIPLES

Although Americans usually agree on abstract democratic principles, they have frequently disagreed on how these should be applied to specific situations. In working out such disagreements, each side tries to persuade the other that it is correct, rather than resorting to force. American history is full of examples of such disagreements, including the protective tariff, national bank, continuation of slavery, regulation of railroads, voting for women, civil rights for minorities, intervention in overseas wars, and abortion. Americans decide such issues by using the democratic process. The will of the majority prevails, unless some constitutional right is affected. In that case, the U.S. Supreme Court has the final word until the Constitution is amended.

A recent example of how Americans can agree on abstract principles but disagree on how they are applied may be found in the area of political reform. Almost all Americans agree on the need for democratic elections. Although the **Federal Election Campaign Act of 1971** and other laws limit the amount that one person or group can contribute directly to an individual political candidate, the costs of waging election campaigns continue to increase. Many Americans support further restrictions on campaign contributions and spending; others oppose such restraints.

AMERICAN GOVERNMENT AND WORLD AFFAIRS

Foreign policy is the conduct of one nation towards other nations. Michigan's High School Test in Social Studies requires you to know about American foreign policy and to be able to evaluate foreign policy decisions.

American Foreign Policy Goals. The main objective of American foreign policy has always been to act according to the **national interest** — what is best for the country. Many factors determine what our leaders believe the national interest to be:

GOALS OF U.S. FOREIGN POLICY

National Security. The highest goal of U.S. foreign policy is to protect our nation's own security. We achieve this through military preparedness and by participating in international organizations like NATO.

Protection of U.S. Citizens And Investments. The United States acts to protect its citizens overseas. For example, in the 1970s, concern for American hostages in Iran had a strong influence on our foreign policy.

Promotion of American Trade. The United States acts to promote the American economy. For example, the promotion of trade has been crucial to the American negotiation of NAFTA.

Promotion of Democracy. The United States actively seeks to spread democracy. For example, during the Cold War, American foreign policy consistently opposed the spread of Communism to other countries.

Promotion of Human Rights and Peace. Our nation supports morality and peace throughout the world, realizing that the fate of every country depends on the survival of the human race. For this reason, the U.S. is a member of the U.N.

Looking at How Foreign Policy Decisions are Made. To implement our foreign policy goals, government leaders make foreign policy decisions. Like any other decision-making process, decision-making in foreign policy involves: (1) selecting goals; (2) weighing alternatives; and (3) choosing a course of action. Here, as an example, we will consider President Kennedy's decision-making during the Cuban Missile Crisis in October 1962, at the height of the Cold War.

✦ **Step 1: What Is the Goal?** The first step is to determine the immediate objective or goal of the policy. Usually the objective will be related to one of the underlying foreign policy goals of the United States.

> An American spy plane observed Soviet technicians constructing missile launching sites in Cuba. President Kennedy was told that within a few days the missiles would be activated.
>
> • **Immediate Objective**: Remove the missiles before they could be activated.
>
> • **Long-Term Goal**: Protect the nation against a nuclear attack.

✦ **Step 2: What Are the Alternatives?** The second step is to examine the various choices available to achieve that goal. Government leaders have to consider the advantages and disadvantages of each option.

> Kennedy and his advisors had a number of options, such as:
>
> • The United States could impose a naval blockade on Cuba.
> • U.S. bombers could destroy the missile sites.
> • The U.S. military could invade Cuba.
> • The United States could do nothing.

✦ **Step 3: What Is the Best Choice Available?** After considering the options, government leaders must eventually make a choice. In order to evaluate the soundness of their decision, you have to decide whether the best alternative was chosen. Did it succeed in reaching the goal? Did the policy assume any unnecessary risks or dangers?

> President Kennedy decided on a naval blockade of Cuba, combined with a threat to invade Cuba. These steps convinced Soviet leaders to withdraw their missiles from Cuba. Although the objective was achieved, some critics claim the risk of nuclear war that Kennedy took was too great.

THE GLOBAL IMPACT OF AMERICAN CONCEPTS OF INDIVIDUAL RIGHTS AND DEMOCRACY

One way that the United States has played an important role in world affairs has been through example. Indeed, American ideals of individual rights and democracy have had a great impact on the world almost from their inception. Many people in other countries have looked at the United States as an ideal society — a model for their own future.

The French Revolution (1798-1799). Thirteen years after the Declaration of Independence, French citizens rebelled against their king and demanded democratic government. French demands of "Liberty, Equality, and Fraternity" were influenced by the American Declaration of Independence.

The Independence of Latin America (1796-1830). Patriots in Latin America were likewise influenced by the American Declaration of Independence when they declared their own liberation from Spain, Portugal, or France.

European Liberalism (1830-1920). European liberals, who favored national self-determination and democracy in place of monarchy, looked to the United States as a model. Alexis de Tocqueville's book *Democracy in America* served as an example of this trend. After World War I, President Woodrow Wilson brought American democratic ideals to Europe by helping to negotiate the Treaty of Versailles and establish new nation-states in Eastern Europe.

Democracy in Asia. In China, **Dr. Sun Yat Sen** was influenced by American democratic ideals when he helped overthrow the Manchu Dynasty in 1911-1912.

Japan was occupied by U.S. forces after World War II. U.S. leaders helped re-write the Japanese constitution, transferring the emperor's political power to the people, and thereby opening the way for Japan to become a free and democratic society. The Philippines, once a colony of the United States, also became an independent, democratic nation after the Second World War.

The Empress Dowager. After 2,500 years of rule by emperors, China became a republic in 1912.

124

The United Nations. Influenced in large part by American ideals, the United Nations adopted the **Universal Declaration of Human Rights** in 1948. It defined those basic rights that members of the United Nations believed should be guaranteed to citizens of all countries. These basic rights included many that were previously spelled out in the American Declaration of Independence and Bill of Rights. For example, the Universal Declaration of Human Rights states that everyone has a right to be free, and that no one should be enslaved or abused by other people.

*The hall where the General Assembly of
the United Nations meets in New York City*

The Spread of Democracy in the 1980s and 1990s. In the 1980s and 1990s, the success of American democracy was influential in the fall of Communism and the spread of democracy throughout Africa and Latin America.

◆ **Soviet Union and Eastern Europe**. In the Soviet Union, Mikhail Gorbachev permitted greater freedom of speech, individual liberty, and democracy, resulting in an end to the Communist dictatorship that had been in power since 1917. The Soviet Union dissolved into a number of separate national states. In Eastern Europe, newly elected democratic governments replaced former Communist dictators.

◆ **Africa and Latin America**. In Africa and Latin America, many military governments and dictators transferred power to freely elected governments. For example, in Chile, Panama, Argentina, and Haiti, military dictatorships were replaced by freely elected democratic governments.

SECTION 2

MAJOR CIVICS TERMS AND CONCEPTS

Use the following graphic organizer as a review to see if you can recall these important terms and concepts in civics.

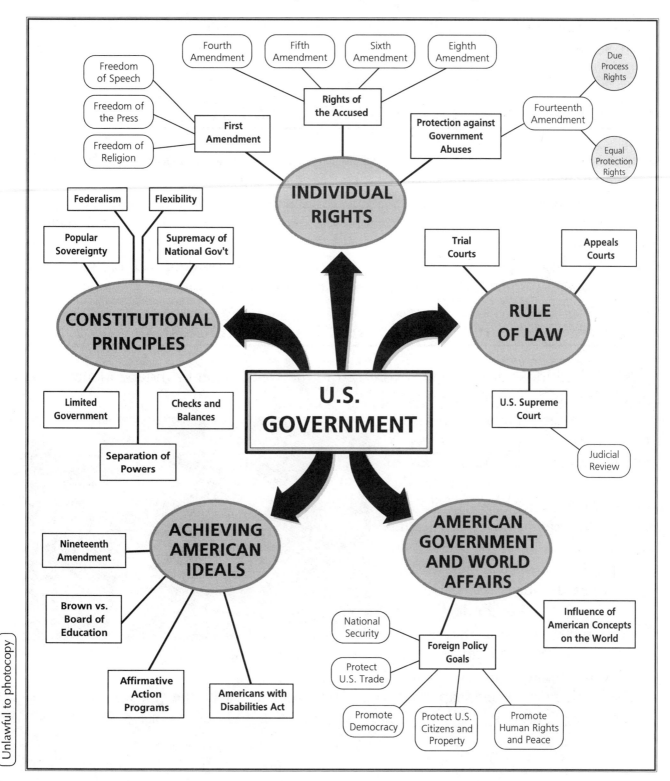

SECTION 3

THE CONTENT STANDARDS FOR CIVICS

It is important for you to understand the main ideas that will be tested on Michigan's High School Test in Social Studies. This section identifies the content standards for civics.

STANDARD III.1: PURPOSES OF GOVERNMENT

This standard focuses on the purposes of American government. You should be able to evaluate how well the federal government serves the purposes for which it was created, and be able to explain the advantages and disadvantages of American federalism. For example, under our federal system, citizens are able to retain control over local matters, while important national issues are resolved by our national government. You should also be able to compare the American system of electing a President with parliamentary systems where a Prime Minister is chosen by members of Parliament.

STANDARD III.2: IDEALS OF AMERICAN DEMOCRACY

This standard looks at the ideals expressed in the Declaration of Independence. You should be able to explain the basic ideas of the Declaration, such as that the purpose of government is to protect individual rights and that citizens can overthrow a government that abuses their rights. You should also be able to explain how the Declaration set a foundation for later American political and civic life, and be able to use the ideas of the Declaration to evaluate the conduct of citizens, political behavior, and government actions. You should especially be able to explain how the ideals of

The signing of the Declaration of Independence, 1776

American democracy are shaped by and help citizens deal with the challenges of diversity in American life, such as racial, religious, regional, and gender-based differences.

STANDARD III.3: DEMOCRACY IN ACTION

This standard explores the role of law and political activity in American society. It looks at how both legal and political processes help Americans to resolve conflicts and reach decisions. You should be able to evaluate the effectiveness of our civil and criminal courts by referring to actual cases. You should also be able to explain how people may agree on abstract democratic principles, like freedom of religion, but disagree on how they should be applied to specific situations, like prayers in school. Finally, you should be able to explain the advantages and disadvantages of hypothetical constitutional amendments that would change or reform our system of democracy.

Protesters in Washington D.C.

STANDARD III.4: AMERICAN GOVERNMENT AND POLITICS

This standard focuses on the organization of American government. You should be able to explain the causes of tension between the branches of government. For example, you should know how the U.S. Supreme Court strikes down laws passed by Congress if it finds them to be unconstitutional. You should also be able to evaluate proposals for government reform, such as campaign finance reform.

STANDARD III.5: AMERICAN GOVERNMENT AND WORLD AFFAIRS

This standard examines international relations. You should be able to describe the influence of American concepts of democracy and individual rights on other parts of the world — such as Eastern Europe in the later 1980s and China at the time of the demonstrations at Tiananmen Square in 1989. You should also be able to evaluate American foreign policy decisions and positions from the point of view of national interests. Finally, you should be able to evaluate the relationship of the United States to international organizations such as NATO and the United Nations.

In China, many Tiananenmen Square protesters were imprisoned or executed.

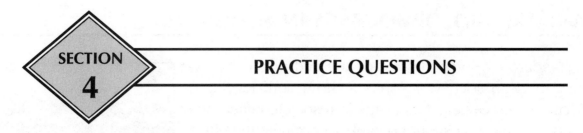

SECTION 4

PRACTICE QUESTIONS

— SELECTED-RESPONSE QUESTIONS —

Directions: Examine the following diagram and use it with what you already know to answer the questions that follow.

THE NATIONAL GOVERNMENT OF THE UNITED STATES

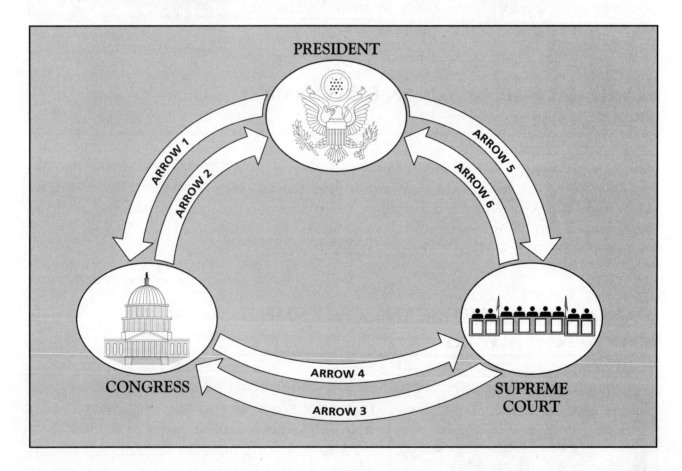

1 Which core democratic value does this diagram BEST illustrate?

  A Federalism

  B Checks and balances

  C Popular sovereignty

  D Individual rights

III.2.HS.2

2 Which BEST explains why the framers of the U.S. Constitution organized our national government as illustrated in the diagram?

  A They wanted to limit the powers of big business.

  B They wished to protect the rights of Americans to worship freely.

  C They sought to prevent one branch of government from becoming too strong.

  D They felt Americans needed a Bill of Rights.

III.1.HS.2

3 Which arrow would identify the power of the President to refuse to sign a bill passed by Congress?

  A Arrow 1

  B Arrow 4

  C Arrow 5

  D Arrow 6

III.4.HS.2

4 Which power might be identified by Arrow 3?

  A The power of the U.S. Supreme Court to declare acts of Congress unconstitutional.

  B The power of the President to appoint ambassadors to foreign nations.

  C The power of the Senate to reject Presidential appointments.

  D The power of the U.S. Congress to override a Presidential veto

III.4.HS.2

5 Which method would be required to change the pattern of organization of the national government as reflected in this diagram?

  A Congress must pass a law, which is signed by the President.

  B Congress and the states must amend the U.S. Constitution.

  C The President must sign an Executive Order.

  D The U.S. Supreme Court must approve the change.

III.4.HS.1

Name _____ Teacher _____

Directions: Read the following passage, and use it with what you already know to answer the questions that follow.

MAPP V. OHIO (1961)

Dollree Mapp was suspected of having illegal gambling equipment in her home.

One day the police broke into her house and conducted a search without a search warrant. The police did not find any gambling equipment, but did discover other materials that were illegal in Ohio. The materials were seized by the police and used as evidence against Ms. Mapp at her trial.

At the trial in Cleveland, Ohio, Ms. Mapp was convicted of possessing illegal materials. Her attorney appealed the conviction to the U.S. Supreme Court, on the grounds that her constitutional rights had been violated.

The Supreme Court's majority opinion was written by Justice Clark. The opinion stated that all evidence used in a court of law must

The room in which the U.S. Supreme Court delivered its decision in Mapp v. Ohio

be obtained legally. Since the police had searched Ms. Mapp's home without a proper warrant, the evidence they found could not be used against her. Justice Clark concluded that "tolerance of shortcut methods in law enforcement impairs its enduring effectiveness."

6 Which power of the U.S. Supreme Court is BEST illustrated by this case?

  A The power to settle disputes between states

  B The power to interpret the U.S. Constitution

  C The power to review acts of Congress

  D The power to hear cases between a state and citizens of another state.

III.1.HS.2

7 On which principle did the U.S. Supreme Court most likely base its decision?

  A Ms. Mapp's free speech rights allowed her to possess the material that was seized.

  B Ms. Mapp was protected from unlawful searches.

  C The police obtained a confession from Ms. Mapp before she was told she could consult a lawyer.

  D An accused person has the right to confront opposing witnesses.

III.2.HS.2

8 If you had been the lawyer representing Ms. Mapp, which document would you MOST likely have referred to in support of your argument?

  A Declaration of Independence

  B Articles of Confederation

  C Bill of Rights

  D The Civil Rights Act of 1964

III.2.HS.2

9 Which core democratic value could Ms. Mapp have used to support her position in this case?

  A Representative government

  B Individual rights

  C Separation of powers

  D Popular sovereignty

III.1.HS.2

10 The U.S. Supreme Court decision in this case reinforces which idea about the powers of government?

  A Some actions are prohibited only to the national government.

  B Some actions are prohibited to local government.

  C Some actions are prohibited only to the state governments.

  D Some actions are prohibited to both the national and state governments.

III.1.HS.2

Name _____ Teacher _____

— CONSTRUCTED-RESPONSE QUESTIONS —

The following section has two constructed-response questions. Read the directions and examine each question carefully before answering.

Directions: You should take about 5 minutes to examine the following diagram and use it with what you already know to complete this task.

THE AMERICAN SYSTEM OF GOVERNMENT

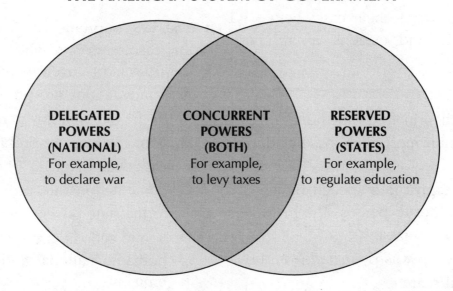

DELEGATED POWERS (NATIONAL)
For example, to declare war

CONCURRENT POWERS (BOTH)
For example, to levy taxes

RESERVED POWERS (STATES)
For example, to regulate education

11 On the lines provided, describe **one advantage** and **one disadvantage** of the system of government shown in the diagram.

Explanation of an advantage of this system of government: _____

_____

_____

_____

Explanation of a disadvantage of this system of government:_____

_____

_____

_____

III.1.HS.1

Name _____ Teacher _____

Directions: You should take about 5 minutes to examine the following diagrams and use them with what you already know to complete this task.

A representative democracy is one in which the will of the people is carried out by their elected representatives. A representative democracy may take one of two forms: Presidential or Parliamentary.

TWO FORMS OF GOVERNMENT

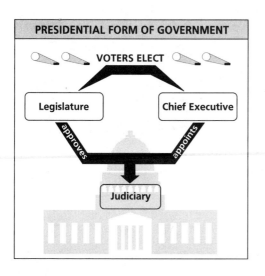
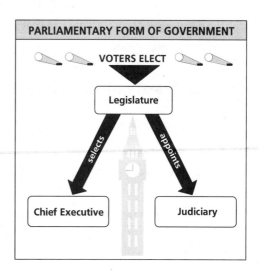

12 On the lines provided, describe two basic differences between these forms of government.

Description of one difference between the Presidential and Parliamentary forms of government: _____

_____

_____

Description of a second difference between the Presidential and Parliamentary forms of government: _____

_____

_____

III.1.HS.3

Name _____ Teacher _____

BENCHMARKS OF THE CIVICS STRAND

Standard III.1: Purposes of Government

III.1.HS.1 Explain advantages and disadvantages of a federal system of government.

III.1.HS.2 Evaluate how effectively the federal government is serving the purposes for which it was created.

III.1.HS.3 Evaluate the relative merits of the American presidential system and parliamentary systems.

Standard III.2: Ideals of American Democracy

III.2.HS.1 Identify the benefits and challenges of diversity in American life.

III.2.HS.2 Use the ideas in the Declaration of Independence to evaluate the conduct of citizens, political behavior, and the practices of government.

Standard III.3: Democracy in Action

III.3.HS.1 Using actual cases, evaluate the effectiveness of civil and criminal courts in the United States.

III.3.HS.2 Explain why people may agree on democratic values in the abstract but disagree when they are applied to specific situations.

III.3.HS.3 Evaluate possible amendments to the Constitution.

Standard III.4: American Government and Politics

III.4.HS.1 Evaluate proposals for reform of the political system.

III.4.HS.2 Analyze causes of tension between the branches of government.

Standard III.5: American Government and World Affairs

III.5.HS.1 Describe the influence of the American concept of democracy and individual rights in the world.

III.5.HS.2 Evaluate foreign policy positions in light of national interests and American values.

III.5.HS.3 Decide what the relationship should be between the United States and international organizations.

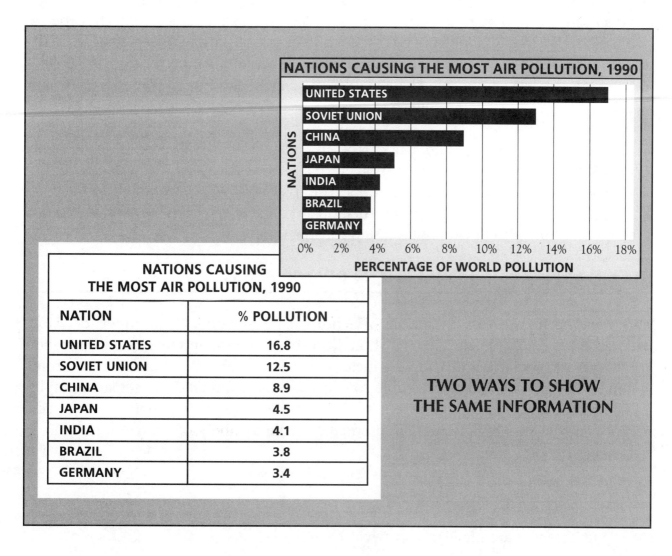

NATIONS CAUSING THE MOST AIR POLLUTION, 1990	
NATION	% POLLUTION
UNITED STATES	16.8
SOVIET UNION	12.5
CHINA	8.9
JAPAN	4.5
INDIA	4.1
BRAZIL	3.8
GERMANY	3.4

**TWO WAYS TO SHOW
THE SAME INFORMATION**

SECTION 1

THE CONTENT STANDARDS FOR INQUIRY

One of the main purposes of social studies is to help prepare young people to become responsible citizens. A responsible citizen must be able to participate in making decisions on important issues facing the community, state, and nation. In order to participate effectively, a person must be knowledgeable about these issues. In the world today, we receive information about such issues in a variety of formats, including line graphs, bar graphs, pie charts, tables, timelines, and maps. These formats have already been described in Chapter 3 of this book.

The inquiry section of the High School Test in Social Studies will examine your ability to interpret information from these various formats, as well as your ability to convert information from one format to another. For example, you may be required to interpret a bar graph and to re-format the information it contains into a table. Following is a description of the skills that will be tested for this standard.

STANDARD V.1: INFORMATION PROCESSING

This standard focuses on the means of acquiring information for informed decision-making as a responsible citizen. You should be able to locate and interpret information about specific social science topics, including information obtained from electronic technologies. You should also be able to organize this information into maps, graphs, and tables. Finally, you should be able to develop generalizations pertaining to specific social science topics by interpreting information from a variety of sources.

Now that you are familiar with what the inquiry strand focuses on, let's look at a typical inquiry question:

SECTION 2

EXAMINING AN INQUIRY QUESTION

Directions: You should take about five minutes to study the following material and use it with what you already know to complete these tasks.

WHAT STATES SPEND ON EDUCATION

Various states spend differing amounts on educating their students. Below is information on this topic.

AVERAGE SPENDING PER PUPIL ON EDUCATION, 1995

STATE	SPENDING PER STUDENT	STATE	SPENDING PER STUDENT
Connecticut	$8,473	Alabama	$4,037
Massachusetts	$6,959	Arkansas	$4,280
New Jersey	$9,677	Mississippi	$3,660
New York	$9,175	Georgia	$4,915
Rhode Island	$7,333	Kentucky	$5,107

Task I

1 Use the information in the tables to make a statement about the *relationship* between the **amount spent on education** and **location** in the U.S.

_____

_____

_____

_____

V.1.HS.1

continued ...

138

TASK II

2 Using the information in the tables, complete the key below the map by shading or cross-hatching each box differently, and labeling the dollar ranges of per-pupil spending for each box. Then shade each state listed in the tables in accordance with the key, and give the map a title.

Title: _____

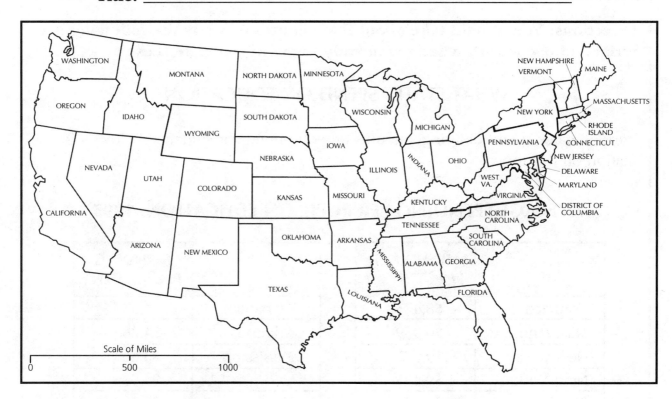

V.1.HS.2

A careful examination of the question shows that there are three parts to deal with:

Let's look at each part separately, to see what is required in presenting an answer.

Name_____ Teacher_____

THE DATA: An inquiry question will always present related information about some topic. In the data presented, there will be **two** things (called *variables*) that deal with the general topic. When one variable changes, it often will have an impact on the other variable. For example, age and height of young people are two variables. Usually, as age increases, the average height of people that age increases also. In our sample question, the general topic and the two variables are as follows:

General Topic: Average education spending per pupil
Variable #1: State
Variable #2: Amount spent per pupil

TASK I: In Task I, you are asked to make a **connection** or to identify a **relationship** between the two variables by answering a constructed-response question. The question tests your ability to see common patterns. You have to look at the specific information for the purpose of making a generalization. A **generalization** is a general statement that identifies a common pattern among several different facts.

In the tables on page 137, you can see that states in the Northeast region (*Connecticut, Massachusetts, New Jersey, New York, and Rhode Island*), have higher spending per pupil on education than states in the South (*Alabama, Arkansas, Mississippi, Georgia and Kentucky*). This question tests your ability to interpret social science information and to make inferences supported by evidence. This information, of course, does not mean that citizens in the South care less about education — it may simply indicate that costs are generally lower in the South than in the Northeast.

TASK II: In Task II, you will be asked to take the information in the data and to **reorganize** it into **another type of data format**. In this question, Task II tested your ability to reorganize the social science information found in the tables into a map. What Task II really tests is your understanding of data, and how different data formats are constructed. Chapter 3, you will recall, has a detailed description of each type of format.

On the following page is a model answer to Task II.

Title: _____AVERAGE SPENDING PER PUPIL ON EDUCATION, 1995_____

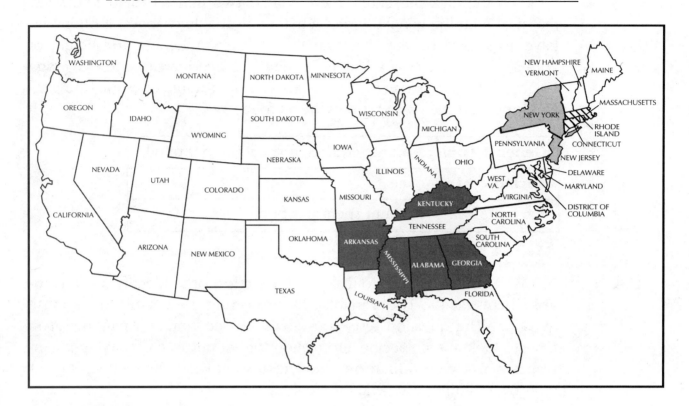

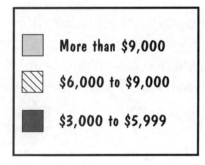

More than $9,000

$6,000 to $9,000

$3,000 to $5,999

SECTION 3

A SAMPLE INQUIRY QUESTION

Let's test your understanding of inquiry questions.
Answer the following sample question.

Directions: You should take about five minutes to study the following material and use it with what you already know to complete these tasks.

The world's population is increasing at a rapid rate. It is estimated that by the year 2025 the population of the world will be about 8 billion people.

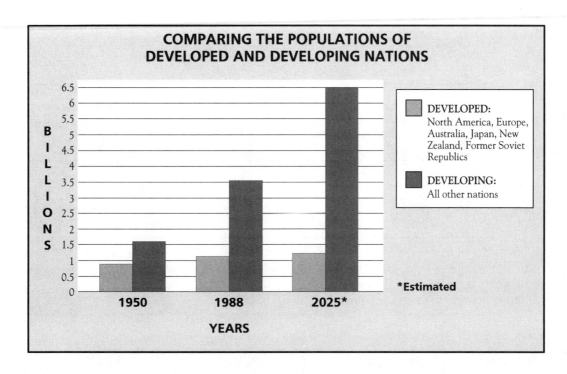

TASK I

1 Study the information in the bar graph. Make a statement about the *relationship* between the **population of developed nations** and the **population of developing nations**.

_____

_____

_____

V.1.HS.3

Name_____ Teacher_____

TASK II

2 Use the information in the bar graph on page 141 to make a line graph comparing the populations of developed and developing nations. In addition, give the graph a title, correctly label each axis, and complete the key.

TITLE: _____

Label: _____

Label: _____

KEY

⸻ =

– – – =

Name_____ Teacher_____

CHAPTER 11

PUBLIC DISCOURSE AND DECISION-MAKING: ANSWERING EXTENDED-RESPONSE QUESTIONS

Local petition drive

Voting by paper ballot on Election Day

Members of the Michigan Militia

EXTENDED-RESPONSE QUESTIONS

The last type of question on the High School Test in Social Studies is known as an **extended-response question**. These questions ask you to write a short essay or letter expressing a position on a public policy issue. There will be two extended-response questions on each test. This chapter will show you how to answer an extended-response question in three steps:

+ First, you will learn what a "public policy issue" is;
+ Second, you will identify *core democratic values*; and
+ Third, you will examine a sample extended-response question.

DEFINING A "PUBLIC POLICY" ISSUE

An **issue** is a topic about which people have different points of view. A **public policy issue** is a matter of concern to an entire community that must be addressed by members of the community. The community could be your town, state, or the nation. Public policy issues often center on whether the government should pass a law or take some other action to solve a problem. Public policy issues are often stated as "should" questions:

+ *Should* parents be allowed to choose which schools their children attend?
+ *Should* Congress make it illegal to import products made by child labor?
+ *Should* the U.S. Constitution be amended to abolish the electoral college?

There is no single "right" or "wrong" side to an issue. People take different positions based on their points of view. When asked to state your position on an issue, you should present the position you think is best. Then you *must* support your position with facts.

THE CORE DEMOCRATIC VALUES

In making decisions about public issues, Americans apply a set of common values. A **value** is something we consider important and worthwhile. We refer to the basic values of American society as the **core democratic values**.

The idea that every person has worth and dignity is the underlying principle behind our core democratic values. American society is based on the notion that the importance of every person should be recognized and respected by others. From this belief springs our devotion to equality, representative government, individual rights, the rule of law, and other core values of American democracy. These values help to unite all Americans.

Our core democratic values originate in two key documents from our history: the **Declaration of Independence** (1776) and the **U.S. Constitution** (1787). These two documents can be thought of as mighty pillars supporting our society. In the Declaration, Americans declared their freedom from Great Britain. The Declaration also announced that there were certain basic truths about people that all governments should recognize. One of these truths was that the purpose of government should be to protect the "life, liberty, and pursuit of happiness" of its citizens.

George Washington presides as the U.S. Constitution is being signed.

The framers of the U.S. Constitution organized our government to allow the national government to pursue its goals while also preserving our individual freedoms. To ensure that the central government did not become too powerful or oppressive, the framers created a federal system of government that divides political power between the federal government and the states. To further discourage the possibility of tyranny, the authors of the Constitution separated political power within the federal government among three branches. Each branch is able to check the others, thus balancing political power among them.

On the next page is a chart listing the core democratic values that will appear on the High School Test in Social Studies. Note that these core democratic values are divided into **Fundamental Beliefs** and **Constitutional Principles** of government. In each extended-response question, you will be asked to refer to at least one of these core democratic values and to show how it supports your position. You should refer to Chapter 9 (Civics) for an explanation of what each of these values means.

Some Core Democratic Values of American Constitutional Democracy

Core democratic values are the fundamental beliefs and constitutional principles of American society. These values unite all Americans. They are expressed in the Declaration of Independence, the United States Constitution, and other significant documents, speeches, and writings of the nation. Below is a list of some core democratic values. **You may use any core democratic value to support your position including those not on this list.** Be sure to explain **how** the value you choose supports the position you take.

Fundamental Beliefs

Life

Liberty

The Pursuit of Happiness

Justice

Equality

Diversity

Truth

Popular Sovereignty

The Common Good

Patriotism

Constitutional Principles

The Rule of Law

Separation of Powers

Representative Government

Checks and Balances

Individual Rights

Freedom of Religion

Federalism

Civilian Control of the Military

<table>
</table>

SECTION 3 — A SAMPLE EXTENDED-RESPONSE QUESTION

Now that you have learned about public policy issues and core democratic values, let's see how they should be used in answering extended-response questions. The following sample question is similar to the extended-response questions that you will encounter on the actual High School Test in Social Studies.

Directions: Read the following information about a public policy issue. Use it with what you already know to complete the tasks that follow. You should take about 20 minutes to complete both Task I and Task II. Task I is a selected-response item and Task II is an extended-response item.

RANDOM DRUG TESTING OF STUDENTS

To discourage illegal drug use by students, the U.S. Congress is considering a bill requiring all schools to conduct random drug testing. If passed, the bill would require some students to provide a blood or urine sample. Each school could test up to 10% of its students each year.

DATA SECTION

PART A — The following study was released by the Survey Research Center of the University of Michigan at Ann Arbor in 1997.

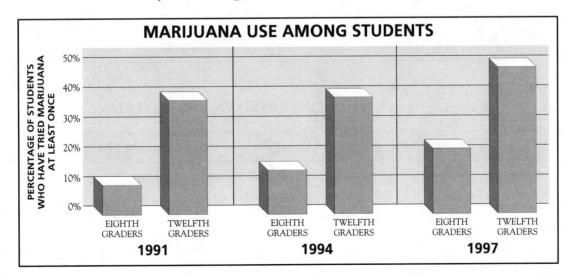

MARIJUANA USE AMONG STUDENTS

PART B

OPINION SURVEY ON THE RANDOM DRUG TESTING OF STUDENTS

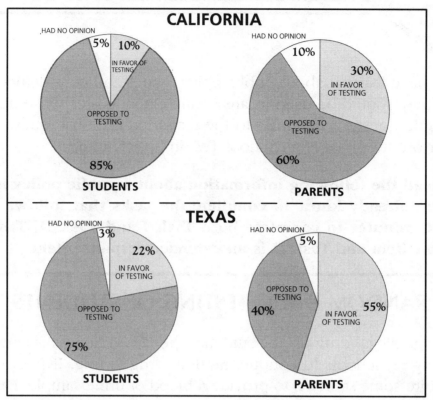

CALIFORNIA

STUDENTS
- HAD NO OPINION 5%
- IN FAVOR OF TESTING 10%
- OPPOSED TO TESTING 85%

PARENTS
- HAD NO OPINION 10%
- IN FAVOR OF TESTING 30%
- OPPOSED TO TESTING 60%

TEXAS

STUDENTS
- HAD NO OPINION 3%
- IN FAVOR OF TESTING 22%
- OPPOSED TO TESTING 75%

PARENTS
- HAD NO OPINION 5%
- OPPOSED TO TESTING 40%
- IN FAVOR OF TESTING 55%

PART C

COMPARING DRUG-USERS WITH NON-USERS

ACCIDENTS:	Drug users are three times more likely to be involved in school or on-the-job accidents than non-users.
ABSENTEEISM:	Drug users are absent from school or work twice as often as non-users.
SICKNESS:	Drug users experience three times the level of sickness as non-users.

PART D

COMMON SOURCES OF ERRORS IN DRUG TESTING

REASON FOR A FALSE READING	HOW OFTEN IT OCCURS
Eating certain foods (e.g. poppy seed bagel) or taking certain medicines (e.g. antihistamines)	5 to 10%
Laboratory error	1 to 5%

COMPLETE THE FOLLOWING TASKS:

Task I: Interpreting Information

Study the information in the Data Section. Which of the following statements best describes the *relationship* between the **time period** and the **percentage of students who have used marijuana at least once**? <u>Be sure to mark your answer on the answer sheet.</u>

A Only the percentage of eighth graders experimenting with marijuana has changed.

B The percentage of students experimenting with marijuana has declined.

C The percentage of students experimenting with marijuana has increased.

D The percentage of students experimenting with marijuana has remained the same.

Task II: Taking a Stand

You will now take a stand on the following public issue: **Should the U.S. Congress pass a law requiring schools to test their students randomly for illegal drug use?** You may either support or oppose random drug testing. Write a letter to your representative in Congress expressing your view. Use information to provide reasons that support your position.

> You will be graded on the following, so be sure your letter includes each of the elements listed below:
>
> * A clear statement of your position.
> * Supporting information using core democratic values of American constitutional democracy. (See page 146 for examples.)
> * Supporting knowledge from history, geography, civics, or economics that you already know. (It is not enough to state only your opinion.)
> * Supporting information from the Data Section.
> * An alternative view and explanation why the alternative position would be a less effective public policy.

Remember to: Use complete sentences.
Explain your reasons in detail.
Write or print neatly on the lines provided.

Should the U.S. Congress pass a law requiring schools to test their students randomly for illegal drug use?

Dear Representative:

_____

_____

_____

_____

_____

_____

_____

_____

_____

_____

_____

_____

_____

_____

_____

_____

_____

_____

Use this checklist to review your letter:

❑ I stated my position clearly.

❑ I supported my position with reference to at least one core democratic value of American constitutional democracy.

❑ I supported my position with knowledge from history, geography, civics, or economics that I already knew.

❑ I supported my position with information from the Data Section.

❑ I stated an alternative view and explained why it would be a less effective public policy.

As you can see from this sample, extended-response questions consist of two main parts: **Task I** and **Task II**. Let's take a closer look at each of these.

ANSWERING THE QUESTION: TASK I

Task I tests your understanding of information in the Data Section. As stated in the previous chapter on Inquiry, Task I asks you to make a **connection** or to see a **relationship** between two variables (*the period of time and the percentage of students who have tried marijuana*). This part of the task tests your ability to see common patterns in specific examples. Let's focus on the pieces of evidence in the Data Section.

✦ **Part A** furnishes a bar graph comparing the percentage of students who have tried marijuana in three different years — 1991, 1994, and 1997.

✦ **Part B** contains pie charts showing how students and parents in California and Texas feel about random drug testing in schools.

✦ **Part C** provides a table comparing drug users with non-drug users, in terms of accidents, absenteeism, and sickness.

✦ **Part D** presents a table showing the two most common sources of errors when drug tests are administered.

Task I specifically tests your understanding of the data in **Part A**. In a study of how many students in the eighth and twelfth grades have experimented with marijuana at least once, it was found that the percentage of students who had tried marijuana had increased between 1991 and 1997 for students in both grades.

Thus **choice C** is correct, since the percentage of both eighth and twelfth graders experimenting with marijuana has increased — from 10% to 22% in eighth grade and from 38% to 49% in twelfth grade. Therefore, the choice stating that "The percentage of students experimenting with marijuana has increased" is correct. All of the other choices are incorrect.

ANSWERING THE QUESTION: TASK II

The second part of the question, found in **Task II,** requires you to take a stand on a public policy issue and to support your position with a written defense. Your answer should:

- ✦ State your own position on the issue

- ✦ State the opposing point of view and explain why you disagree with it

- ✦ Support your position with one of the core democratic values

- ✦ Support your position with information from the Data Section

- ✦ Support your position with additional information from your knowledge of social studies

WRITING YOUR ANSWER

Your first step in answering Task II must be to decide your own position on the issue. Let's examine how this can be done.

DECIDING YOUR POSITION

One simple way to decide your own position is to set up a decision-making model. You must compare the advantages or benefits of the proposal in the question with its disadvantages or costs. After weighing the costs and benefits, you should then make your decision based on what you think is best. You might briefly jot down these points or merely think about it.

> **Advantages or Benefits**. A proposal is often advantageous if it helps to deal with a significant problem. Here, drug testing might help reduce student use of drugs. This would benefit society, since use of drugs leads to health problems, poor work habits, absenteeism, and crime. In order to help solve a problem, however, a proposal must be effective. Opponents of proposals often argue that they will not really help deal with the problem. For example, opponents of drug testing would probably claim that it does not really work in reducing drug use.

> **Disadvantages or Costs**. A proposal may have disadvantages that outweigh its benefits. For example, a proposal may be expensive to adopt, or it may threaten individual rights, invade privacy, or treat some groups unequally. When considering a proposal, always take into

account its costs — financial, social, and moral. Is there another proposal that can achieve the same objective at less cost? If so, then that alternative proposal might be better.

USING THE 6-S APPROACH

Once you have decided your position, you are ready to answer the extended-response question. Although there are many ways to go about it, one suggested method is to use the **"6-S"** approach. In this method, each "S" represents a different element that your answer must include.

State your position.

State the opposing viewpoint and explain why you disagree with it.

Select a Core Democratic Value to support your opinion.

Support your position with evidence from the Data Section.

Support your position with evidence from your social studies knowledge.

Summarize your argument.

Let's see how using the "6-S" method can bring all of these factors together into a logical, well-organized answer.

State your Position

You should begin your letter or essay with a clear statement of your position. You can often state your position by simply restating the issue in the question — either affirmatively or negatively. For example,

> *"I support the bill before Congress requiring random drug testing by schools."*

or

> *"I oppose the bill before Congress requiring random drug testing by schools."*

State the Opposing Viewpoint and Explain Why You Disagree with It

Next, you should identify an opposing point of view. In order to do this, think of the advantages and disadvantages you thought of when you first decided your position on the issue. Mention one of the reasons used by people who disagree with your own view.

For example, assume that you decided to *oppose* random drug testing of students. Think about why some people might favor such testing. One reason they might favor testing is to reduce the high costs to society of drug use: students miss classes, do not learn, and may even become involved in crime. You should state this position as the next part of your answer. You might also attempt to show any logical inconsistency or flaw in that argument; otherwise, you can attempt to refute it later in the rest of your answer.

> *"Many people favor random drug testing in school because it sends a clear message to students that illegal drug use will not be tolerated under any circumstances. However, I do not agree with this argument because there is no proof that random drug testing really works to reduce drug use."*

Select a Core Democratic Value

Now you must make a transition to the next part of your essay, where you will explain why you support your own point of view. We suggest that you start by supporting your position with one of the core democratic values. However, the next three sections can be in any order you choose, based upon the question and your own ideas.

Somewhere in your answer, your position must be supported by a specific core democratic value. Be sure that you both **identify** the core democratic value **by name** *and* **relate** it to your position. Although a long list of core democratic values will be presented to you on the test (*see page 146*), most issues will focus on six main values.

1. **INDIVIDUAL RIGHTS AND LIBERTY.** If the question deals with limiting the freedom of individuals, you can refer to this core democratic value. You must however, identify the *specific* individual right to which you refer — such as freedom of speech, freedom of religion, or the right to privacy.

> In this case, you could say that requiring a student to submit a urine or blood sample is a violation of a student's right to privacy — part of our legacy of individual liberty. You might say that such testing in public schools might also violate the Fourth Amendment, since the government should not be able to "search" individuals without cause.

2. **EQUALITY.** The Declaration of Independence asserts that "all men are created equal." The Fourteenth Amendment to the U.S. Constitution states that all Americans must be treated equally under the law. If the question deals with treating some groups differently than others without good reason — especially on the basis of race, religion, age, or gender — you might refer to this core democratic value.

> You might say that drug testing unfairly penalizes students. Drug use among students may be no greater than among young workers or other social groups, yet students are being singled out for highly invasive tests.

3. **JUSTICE.** If the question deals with criminal penalties or taking away property rights, then the core democratic value of justice may be involved.

> An argument might be made that drug testing by schools violates the Fourth Amendment, which only allows the government to search someone when it has a reasonable suspicion. Opponents of drug testing could argue that it is unjust to subject all students, most of whom do not use drugs, to invasive tests.

4. **REPRESENTATIVE GOVERNMENT**. We elect our officials to represent our interests in government. Government officials are supposed to consider what the majority of the people who elect them want done, subject to the rights of the minority and their own judgment of what is best.

> You could refer to the survey in the Data Section which shows that most parents in California oppose testing. Since these voters oppose it, it would be contrary to our system of representative government to impose it on them.

5. **THE COMMON GOOD**. Our democratic society tries to do what is best for the community. Therefore, if the question suggests a proposal that you think would benefit the community, you can support your position with this core democratic value. Your argument might be strengthened if you explained how the common good sometimes conflicts with the interests of certain individuals.

> Any program that reduces student drug use benefits society by reducing crime, lowering health costs, and improving learning. You might therefore support drug testing since it serves to benefit the common good.

Sometimes core democratic values may come into conflict. Even though drug testing promotes the common good, you might still oppose testing on the grounds of individual rights.

6. **FEDERALISM**. Under our system of federalism, the federal government deals with issues of national concern, such as foreign policy, protection from foreign invasion, and interstate commerce. The specific powers of the federal government in these areas are listed in the U.S. Constitution.

Other concerns, such as local education, transportation, or safety standards, are generally regulated by state government. This division of powers prevents the national government from becoming too strong or too weak and gives state residents a greater degree of control over their own lives.

> You might say that random drug testing is best handled by each state government or by individual school districts rather than by our national government. In some places, testing may not be necessary. In others, parents might want to exercise control over how it is done. According to the Data Section, for example, Texas parents support testing, but California parents do not. If you favor drug testing, you might say that drug use is a national problem requiring action by the federal government. The federal government is permitted to act under our Constitution, because illegal drugs affect interstate commerce.

Support Your Position with Evidence from the Data Section

You must also use information from the Data Section to support your point of view. Again, be sure to identify this part of your answer. For example, **Part D** of the Data Section indicates that drug testing sometimes leads to inaccurate results. You could use this fact to argue that testing would be very unfair to those students who are given these mistaken results. Therefore, you might conclude that we should think of other ways to fight drug use in schools.

Support Your Position with Your Social Studies Knowledge

To support your position using your social studies knowledge, keep in mind some of the basic concepts of geography, history, economics, and civics. For example:

Geography. Look at the situation in the question. Are any of the five themes of geography — location, movement, place, human-environment interaction, and region — involved? If so, identify which theme and show how it is related to the question. For example, we know from the study of geography that people are influenced by their environment. You might mention how people might be affected by the proposed policy change.

History. To use historical knowledge, you should consider if you have ever studied a past situation that relates to the public issue in the question. Here you might refer to the outlawing of alcohol in the 1920s during Prohibition. This policy was largely ineffective. Attempts to control students' use of drugs might prove similarly ineffective and simply encourage students to cheat when they give their samples, or to take drugs except when testing is performed.

Economics. Again, start by thinking carefully about the issue in the question. If it involves spending government funds, think about how the government will have to raise the money through taxes. You might also refer to the idea of "opportunity cost" — since every decision to buy something involves some opportunity costs. What might the government give up towards solving other problems, if it spends money solving one problem? For example, by spending money on drug testing, the government might have less money available to reduce class sizes. This would be one of the opportunity costs of drug testing.

Civics. As always, start by looking at the issue in the question and the evidence in the Data Section. Will the local, state, or national government be involved? If so, mention what the role of the government will be in addressing the issue. Does this branch of government have the power, under our Constitution, to take on this role? It is especially helpful to recall that one of the main roles of government is to protect individuals from harm. However, you cannot use your reference to a core democratic value to fulfill the requirement that you use your background social studies knowledge.

Summarize your Arguments

At the end of your response, you should signal closure to the reader by restating your position on the issue. For example:

> *"As a result of the arguments I have presented in this letter, I feel that Congress should not pass a bill requiring schools to test their students randomly for drugs."*

A SAMPLE ANSWER

What follows is a sample answer that a student might have written to answer this question. Notice how the answer is framed to follow the "**6-S**" approach you just read about. In addition, notice that the answer does not use bullets or outlining. In writing your answer, you may **not** use an outline form. To receive credit, each point provided in your answer must be made by using full sentences.

Dear Representative:

I believe that the U.S. Congress should not pass a law requiring schools to randomly test their students for illegal drug use.

> **State your position**

Many people favor random drug testing in schools, since it sends a clear message to students that illegal drug use will not be tolerated. However, I do not agree with this argument because there is no proof that random drug testing actually works to reduce drug use.

> **State and refute the opposing viewpoint**

There are many reasons why I oppose drug testing in schools. The most important reason is that it violates a student's individual rights — a core democratic value. The individual right being violated is a student's right to privacy. Students would have to allow someone to take a blood sample, or be required to submit a specimen of their urine so the school could monitor drug use. Many students will find this humiliating.

> **Select a core democratic value to support your position**

Part B of the Data Section shows that most students in two states oppose testing. Students should not be subjected to something against their will, when they have done nothing wrong. Part A of the Data Section shows most high school seniors have never even tried marijuana. Why should all students then be subjected to such invasive tests?

> **Select supporting evidence from the Data Section**

If we look at American history, we see that policies that attempt to force people to do things can often backfire. In the 1770s, the British imposed taxes on the American colonists against their will. Eventually, this policy led the colonists to rebel. I think many students will also refuse to cooperate, making enforcement difficult. There are better ways to fight drug use in schools, such as more drug awareness programs.

> **Select supporting evidence from your social studies knowledge**

As a result of the arguments I have presented in this letter, I believe that Congress should not pass a bill requiring schools to conduct random drug tests of their students.

> **Summarize your positon**

Sincerely yours,

_____
(Sign your name)

REMEMBER: Use this basic framework in writing your answer to **any** extended-response question.

CHAPTER 12

A PRACTICE HIGH SCHOOL TEST IN SOCIAL STUDIES

You have now reviewed what you need to know to do well on Michigan's High School Test in Social Studies. At this point, you are ready to take a practice test.

You should take the following test under "test conditions." This means taking the entire test in a quiet room. Complete the test in two separate sessions, as indicated. This will give you a feeling for what the actual test will be like. Taking this practice test will help to reduce any anxiety you might have about the real test.

The practice test will also help you to identify areas that you may still need to study and review. For example, after taking the test you may find you had problems answering selected-response questions on history or extended-response questions on public policy issues. In that case, you should review the sections of this book focusing on those types of questions.

Good luck on this practice test!

DAY ONE: SOCIAL STUDIES ASSESSMENT

Instructions to the Student

There are three types of questions on this test: **selected-response, constructed-response**, and **extended-response**.

- **Selected-response** questions will ask you first to read a passage, map, chart, or table. After studying this prompt, read the questions and choose the best answer from among four answer choices.

- **Constructed-response** questions will ask you to explain a conclusion, provide examples, complete a chart, interpret information, or give a reason for an answer you have given.

- **Extended-response** questions require you to write an answer that is more detailed and requires more thinking. These items ask you to interpret information from a set of data on a hypothetical policy issue, identify a relationship presented in the Data Section, take a position for or against the policy, give reasons supporting your position, and provide a reason why an alternative position would be a less effective public policy.

Use the separate answer sheet *(see page 199)* to mark your choices for the **selected-response** questions. Fill in the circle for your choice on the answer sheet. Remember to fill in the circle completely and cleanly, erasing any stray lines or marks.

Space is provided in the test section for you to write your answers to **constructed-response** and **extended-response** items.

Read all directions for these items carefully.

If you finish early, you may check your work for Day One **only**. Do **not** go ahead and work on the Day Two section of this test.

Geography

Directions: Read the following table of information and use it with what you already know to answer the questions that follow.

CATEGORY	United States	Cuba	Bangladesh	Iraq	Japan
Amount Spent on Defense	4.2% of GDP	4% of GDP	1.7% of GDP	75% of GDP	1% of GDP
Living in Cities	75%	74%	16%	12%	78%
Amount of Arable Land	20%	23%	67%	70%	13%
Number of Doctors	1 per 391 people	1 per 231 people	1 per 5,624 people	1 per 1,922 people	1 per 566 people
Number of Telephones	1 per 1.7 persons	1 per 31 persons	1 per 336 persons	1 per 29 persons	1 per 2.1 persons
Major Religions	Catholic and Protestant	Catholic	Muslim	Muslim	Shinto and Buddhist

Geography

1 In which two countries do farmers probably play the most important role in the economy?

   A United States and Cuba
   B Bangladesh and Iraq
   C Cuba and Japan
   D United States and Iraq

   II.1.HS.1

2 Which countries are probably BEST able to compete in a global economy by selling high-technology goods?

   A Cuba and the United States
   B Bangladesh and Cuba
   C Iraq and Japan
   D United States and Japan

   II.4.HS.3

3 Which factor might BEST explain Iraq's defense expenditures?

   A Iraq's leader holds power through his control of the military.
   B The leaders of Iraq believe in a policy of passive resistance.
   C Iraq is a Muslim nation that does not believe in war.
   D The Constitution of Iraq bars the country from spending on its military.

   II.5.HS2

4 The citizens of which two nations in the table would MOST likely want to visit religious places in Saudi Arabia?

   A Cuba and Iraq
   B Iraq and Japan
   C Iraq and Bangladesh
   D Bangladesh and Japan

   II.1.HS.1

5 According to the table, which nation must achieve the most before it can join the club of "developed" nations?

   A Cuba
   B Bangladesh
   C Iraq
   D Japan

   II.3.HS.1

Geography

Directions: Look at the following map and use it with what you already know to answer the questions that follow.

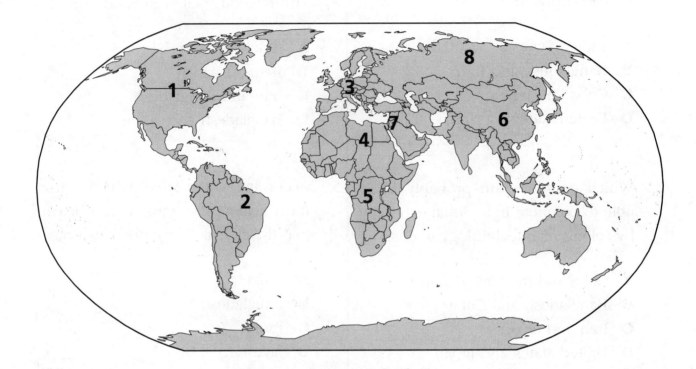

6 Which of the following is the MOST serious environmental problem confronting Areas 1 and 3?

A Cutting down rain forests
B Torrential monsoons
C Desertification
D Industrial pollution

II.1.HS.1

7 Which of the following has recently been an important issue in Area 2?

A Increased ethnic conflict since the fall of Communism
B The cutting down of rain forests to increase national wealth
C Increasing desertification due to global warming
D The rise of Islamic fundamentalism

II.2.HS.1

8 What is one of the MAJOR obstacles to peace and order in Area 7?

A Competition among oil-importers and oil-exporters
B Hostility between Israelis and Palestinians
C Conflicts between Catholics and Protestants
D Israeli ambitions to control the Suez Canal

II.4.HS.4

9 Which of the following approaches has been MOST successful in encouraging economic development in Areas 2, 3, and 6?

A Planned economies directed by central government officials
B Borrowing investment capital from developing nations
C High tariffs to protect local manufacturers
D Free market economies open to foreign investment

II.3.HS.1

10 What was one of the MAIN causes leading to important political changes in Area 8?

A The failure of economic reforms
B A successful coup led by student dissenters
C The decision to establish a free trade organization
D The withdrawal of foreign military forces

II.4.HS.4

Geography

Directions: You should take about 5 minutes to examine the following graphic organizer and use it with what you already know to complete this task.

Recently, social scientists from all over the world gathered to discuss problems facing humankind.

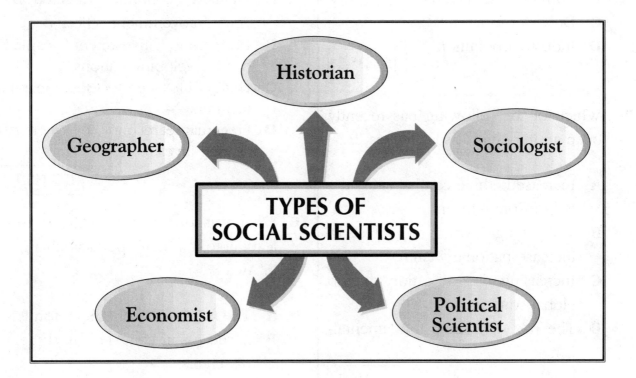

Here are some of the problems they discussed:

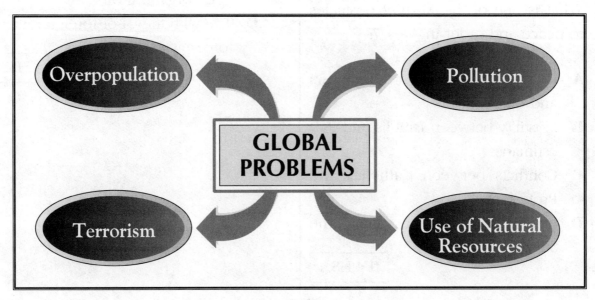

Geography

11 On the lines provided, select **two** problems shown on the graphic organizer. For each problem selected, describe how any one of the social scientists would look at that problem.

First problem selected: _____

What elements or details of the problem a[n] _____ *(social scientist)*

would focus on: _____

_____

_____

_____

_____

Second problem selected: _____

What elements or details of the problem a[n] _____ *(social scientist)*

would focus on: _____

_____

_____

_____

_____

_____

II.1.HS.1

Name _____ Teacher _____

History

Directions: Read the following chart and use it with what you already know to answer the questions that follow.

Historians often divide the continuous stream of events into "historical periods." The following chart shows one way historians have divided the last 130 years of American history.

U.S. HISTORICAL PERIODS, 1870 TO PRESENT

TIME PERIOD 1 (1870-1890)	This period was characterized by the Industrial Revolution, which brought about great increases in the scale of production. Railroads opened the interior of the United States for settlement, speeded up industrialization, and linked production centers to large city markets.
TIME PERIOD 2 (1890-1920)	This period was characterized by the rise of corporations, a flood of arriving immigrants, and government reforms. In foreign affairs, the United States emerged as a nation with global interests. Americans were eventually dragged into a world war.
TIME PERIOD 3 (1920-1945)	This period began with postwar prosperity, but later experienced a severe economic slowdown characterized by high unemployment, increased business failures, and a loss of business profits. It ended with a devastating world war.
TIME PERIOD 4 (1946-1963)	This period saw a rivalry between the world's two Superpowers following World War II. The two Superpowers competed with each other to spread their way of life to other nations.
TIME PERIOD 5 (1964-present)	This period witnessed Americans fighting a war in Asia, the birth of new social programs to help the disadvantaged, and a revolution in computers. As Americans adjusted to new technology, the U.S. lost many jobs, especially in manufacturing.

12 Which was a MAJOR cause leading to the economic slowdown referred to in Time Period 3?

A The founding of Standard Oil Company of America
B The New York Stock Market Crash
C The start of New Deal programs
D Germany's invasion of Poland

I.1.HS.2

13 During Time Period 3, a U.S. President attempted to fight a severe economic depression by providing loans to businesses. What alternative policy did the very next U.S. President believe was a better course of action?

A Depend on charitable organizations for relief
B Rely on private corporations to help the needy
C Create jobs through goverment public works programs
D Permit the economic crisis resolve itself by doing nothing

I.4.HS.1

14 Which statement BEST explains the way the chart is organized?

A Time periods are grouped by centuries.
B Time periods are often organized by common events, characteristics, or circumstances.
C American time periods often parallel the administrations of certain U.S. Presidents.
D Time periods are mainly influenced by social events.

I.1.HS.2

15 Which statement about the war diary of General Dwight Eisenhower would be MOST accurate?

A It provides a primary source about events that took place in Time Period 3.
B It provides a secondary source about events that took place in Time Period 3.
C It provides a secondary source about events that took place in Time Period 5.
D It provides a primary source about events that took place in Time Period 5.

I.1.HS.2

16 What major problem faced the United States during Time Period 5?

A Americans were protesting against the constitutional prohibition on alcohol.
B Americans could not defeat the North Vietnamese and Viet Cong.
C The Great Depression led to massive unemployment.
D Women were denied to right to vote.

I.3.HS.3

History

Directions: Read the following passage and use it with what you already know to answer the questions that follow.

FRANKLIN D. ROOSEVELT'S FIRST INAUGURAL ADDRESS — MARCH 1933

Values have shrunken to fantastic levels; taxes have risen; our ability to pay has fallen; government of all kinds is faced by serious curtailment of income; the means of exchange are frozen in the currents of trade; the withered leaves of industrial enterprise lie on every side; farmers find no markets for their produce; the savings of many years in thousands of families are gone. Most important, a host of unemployed citizens face the grim problem of existence.

This nation asks for action, and action now. Our greatest primary task is to put people back to work. This is no unsolvable problem if we face it wisely and courageously. It can be accomplished in part by direct recruiting by the government itself, treating the task as we would treat the emergency of a war, but at the same time, through this employment, accomplishing greatly needed projects to stimulate and reorganize the use of our natural resources ...

President Roosevelt leaves after delivering his inaugural speech.

The task can be helped by the definite efforts to raise the values of agricultural products and with this power to purchase the output of our cities. It can be helped by preventing ... the tragedy of the growing loss through foreclosure of our small homes and our farms ... It can be helped by the unifying of relief activities which today are often scattered, uneconomical and unequal. It can be helped by national planning for the supervision of all forms of transportation and of communications and other utilities which have a definite public character.

17 What situation was President Franklin D. Roosevelt reacting to in this Inaugural Address?

  A Passage of a high protective tariff

  B Rise of dictators in Europe

  C Widespread unemployment and business failures

  D The Japanese surprise attack on Pearl Harbor

I.1.HS.2

18 Which action by President Roosevelt BEST illustrated his attempt to deal with the problem identified in the second sentence of the second paragraph?

  A Establishment of the Civilian Conservation Corps and other public works programs

  B Introduction of the Social Security Act creating pensions for retired workers

  C The attempt to increase the size of the Supreme Court from nine to fifteen justices

  D Passage of the Wagner Act protecting the right of labor unions to bargain collectively with employers

I.3.HS.1

19 Which of the following groups would have been MOST critical of the suggestions outlined in this speech?

  A unemployed factory workers

  B owners of railroads and utilities

  C western farmers

  D labor union leaders

I.1.HS.2

20 What was a major effect of the programs that President Roosevelt announced in this speech?

  A A reduction in the number of government employees

  B An expansion in the economic role of the federal government

  C A transfer of power from the federal government to the states

  D A significant increase in American foreign aid

I.2.HS.1

21 Which later President of the United States adopted domestic goals most similar to those announced in this speech?

  A Lyndon B. Johnson

  B Richard M. Nixon

  C Ronald Reagan

  D George Bush

I.4.HS.3

History

Directions: You should take about 5 minutes to read the following passage and use it with what you already know to complete this task.

In 1947, President Truman announced the **Truman Doctrine,** declaring that the United States would provide aid to Greece and Turkey to prevent Communists from taking over the governments of those countries.

Later that same year, the United States announced the **Marshall Plan**, giving billions of dollars to Western European nations to help them rebuild their war-torn economies.

In 1948, the Western Allies merged their zones of occupation in Germany. The Soviets reacted by closing all highway and rail links to Berlin. In what became known as the **Berlin Airlift**, Western allies began a massive airlift to feed and supply the city.

In 1949, the United States, Canada, and ten Western European countries formed the **North Atlantic Treaty Organization** (NATO) to protect Western Europe from Communist aggression. The Soviet Union responded in 1955 by creating the **Warsaw Pact** with its Eastern European allies.

In 1961, Soviet leader Khrushchev ordered construction of the **Berlin Wall** between East and West Berlin to prevent East Germans from escaping into West Germany. For the next 28 years, the wall served as a constant reminder of the Cold War.

22 In the graphic provided below, construct a timeline of the **bolded** events. Choose a title for the timeline, and explain why you selected that title.

Title: _____

Explanation of your title: _____

_____

_____

I.1.HS.1

Inquiry and Decision Making

Directions: Read the following information about a public policy issue. Use it with what you already know to complete the tasks that follow. You should take about 20 minutes to complete both Task I and Task II. Task I is a selected-response item and Task II is an extended-response item.

CAPITAL PUNISHMENT

Although 4,291 executions have been carried out in the United States since 1930, imposition of the death penalty remains a hotly contested issue among Americans. Some Americans have proposed amending the Constitution to abolish capital punishment. Examine the following information about this issue.

DATA SECTION

PART A

SELECTED STATISTICS ON EXECUTIONS IN THE U.S., 1976-1998

Number of Executions	486
Inmates on Death Row Freed for Wrongful Conviction	74

Source: U.S. News & World Report

PART B

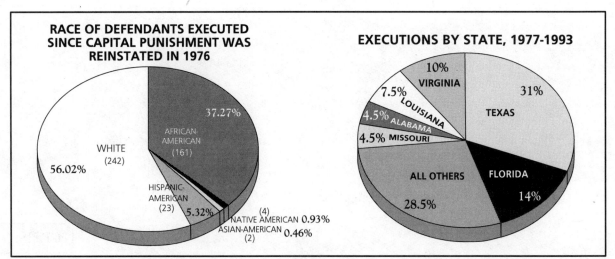

Source: NAACP Legal Defense and Educational Fund, 1998

**PART
C**

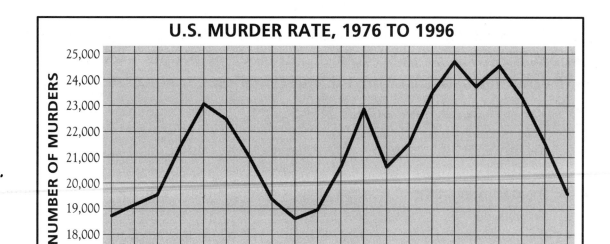

Source: Federal Bureau of Investigation

**PART
D**

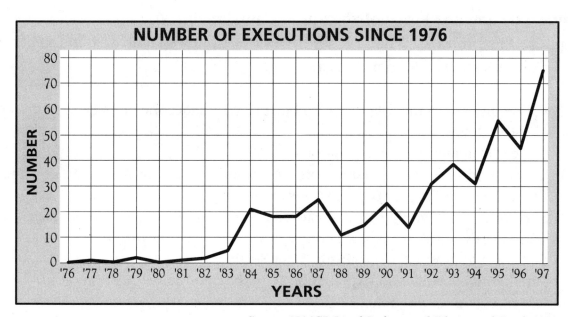

Source: NAACP Legal Defense and Educational Fund, 1998

Inquiry and Decision Making

COMPLETE THE FOLLOWING TASKS:

Task I: Interpreting Information

23 Study the information in the Data Section. Which of the following statements best describes the *relationship* between the **number of people executed** and the **number of murders committed in the United States since 1976**? <u>Be sure to mark your answer on the answer sheet.</u>

A As the number of executions has increased, the number of murders has decreased.

B An increasing number of executions has deterred many criminals from committing murders.

C As the number of executions have increased, the number of murders have increased.

D There is no consistent correlation between the number of executions and the number of murders.

Task II: Taking a Stand

24 You will now take a stand on the following public issue: **Should the U.S. Constitution be amended to abolish capital punishment?** You may either support or oppose this proposal. Write a letter to your local newspaper. Use information to provide reasons that support your position.

You will be graded on the following, so be sure your letter includes each of the elements listed below:
- A clear statement of your position.
- Supporting information using core democratic values of American constitutional democracy. *(See page 146 for examples.)*
- Supporting knowledge from history, geography, civics, or economics that you already know. *(It is not enough to state only your opinion.)*
- Supporting information from the Data Section.
- An alternative view and explanation why the alternative position would be a less effective public policy.

Inquiry and Decision Making

Remember to: Use complete sentences.

Explain your reasons in detail.

Write or print neatly on the lines provided.

Should the U.S. Constitution be amended to abolish capital punishment?

Dear Editor-in-Chief:

_____

_____

_____

_____

_____

_____

_____

_____

_____

_____

_____

_____

_____

_____

_____

(continued...)

Inquiry and Decision Making

_____

_____

_____

_____

_____

_____

_____

_____

_____

_____

_____

_____

_____

_____

_____

Use this checklist to review your letter.

- ❑ I stated my position clearly.
- ❑ I supported my position with reference to at least one core democratic value of American constitutional democracy.
- ❑ I supported my position with knowledge from history, geography, civics, or economics that I already knew.
- ❑ I supported my position with information from the Data Section.
- ❑ I stated an alternative view and explained why it would be a less effective public policy.

STOP

Name _____ Teacher _____

Instructions

DAY TWO: SOCIAL STUDIES ASSESSMENT

Instructions to the Student

There are three types of questions on this test: **selected-response, constructed-response**, and **extended-response**.

- **Selected-response** questions will ask you first to read a passage, map, chart, or table. After studying this prompt, read the questions and choose the best answer from among four answer choices.

- **Constructed-response** questions will ask you to explain a conclusion, provide examples, complete a chart, interpret information, or give a reason for an answer you have given.

- **Extended-response** questions require you to write an answer that is more detailed and requires more thinking. These items ask you to interpret information from a set of data on a hypothetical policy issue, identify a relationship presented in the Data Section, take a position for or against the policy, give reasons supporting your position, and provide a reason why an alternative position would be less effective public policy.

Use the separate answer sheet to mark your choice for the **selected-response** questions. Fill in the circle for your choice on the answer sheet. Remember to fill in the circle completely and cleanly, erasing any stray lines or marks.

Space is provided in the test section for you to write your answers to **constructed-response** and **extended-response** items.

Read all directions for these items carefully.

If you finish early, you may check your work for Day Two **only**. Do **not** work on the Day One section of this test.

Civics

Directions: Examine the following diagram and use it with what you already know to answer the questions that follow:

THE GOALS OF U.S. FOREIGN POLICY

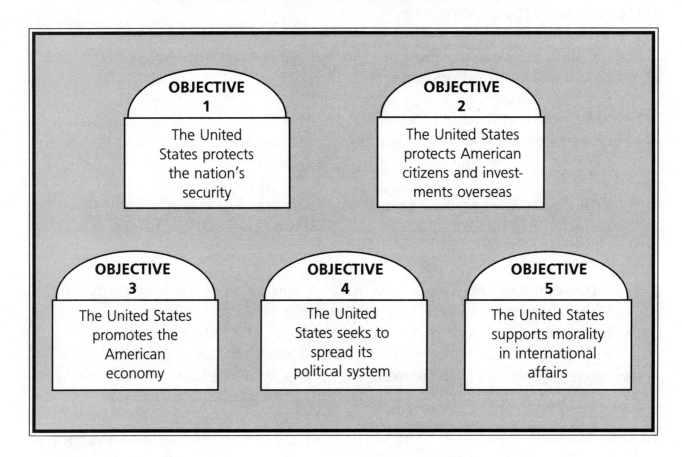

OBJECTIVE 1
The United States protects the nation's security

OBJECTIVE 2
The United States protects American citizens and investments overseas

OBJECTIVE 3
The United States promotes the American economy

OBJECTIVE 4
The United States seeks to spread its political system

OBJECTIVE 5
The United States supports morality in international affairs

Civics

25 Under our federal system of government, which two parts of government are PRIMARILY responsible for carrying out the foreign policy objectives listed in the diagram?

A The President and the U.S. Supreme Court

B The U.S. Supreme Court and the U.S. Congress

C The President and the governors of the 50 states

D The President and the U.S. Congress

III.1.HS.1

26 Which foreign policy objective did U.S. leaders primarily seek to achieve in entering into the North American Free Trade Agreement (NAFTA)?

A Objective 1 **C** Objective 3

B Objective 2 **D** Objective 4

III.5.HS.2

27 Which foreign policy objective does the U.S. pursue when it participates in the United Nations World Health Organization and the United Nations Educational, Scientific, and Cultural Organization?

A Objective 1 **C** Objective 3

B Objective 2 **D** Objective 5

III.5.HS.3

28 Which is the BEST example of the pursuit of foreign policy Objective 4?

A President Eisenhower broke off relations with Cuba after it nationalized American-owned properties.

B President Wilson asked Congress to declare war against Germany in order to "make the world safe for democracy."

C President Carter broke off diplomatic relations with Iran when Iranian terrorists captured the U.S. Embassy in Teheran, Iran.

D President Bush traveled to Tokyo in an attempt to improve the U.S. balance of trade with Japan.

III.5.HS.2

29 What common goal do all of the foreign policy objectives listed on the diagram seek to achieve?

A Attack aggressive nations before they attack us

B Avoid alliances with other nations

C Serve the national interests of the U.S.

D Oppose all undemocratic governments

III.5.HS.2

Civics

Directions: Read the following passage and use it with what you already know to answer the questions that follow.

THE SENECA FALLS CONVENTION

Excerpt from a resolution passed by the Seneca Falls Convention in New York in 1848:

"We hold these truths to be self-evident: that all men and women are created equal; that they are endowed by their Creator with certain inalienable rights; that among these are life, liberty, and the pursuit of happiness; that to secure these rights governments are instituted, deriving their just powers from the consent of the governed. Whenever any form of government becomes destructive of these ends, it is the right of those who suffer from it to refuse allegiance to it, and to insist upon the institution of a new government, laying its foundation on such principles, and organizing its powers in such form, as to them shall seem most likely to effect their safety and happiness ...

The history of mankind is a history of repeated injuries ... on the part of man toward woman, having in direct object the establishment of an absolute tyranny over her. To prove this, let facts be submitted to a candid world. He has never permitted her to exercise her inalienable right to the elective franchise. He has compelled her to submit to laws in the formation of which she had no voice ...

Resolved, that it is the duty of the women in this country to secure to themselves their sacred right to the elective franchise ..."

30 Which earlier document in American history provided the inspiration for the ideas expressed in this document?

A Articles of Confederation
B Declaration of Independence
C Bill of Rights
D Gettysburg Address

III.2.HS.2

31 The ideas expressed in this document later gave rise to which political reform movement in America?

A Granger Movement
B Populist Movement
C Progressive Movement
D Suffrage Movement

III.4.HS.1

32 Which core democratic value represents the central theme of this document?

A Rule of Law
B Federalism
C Separation of Powers
D Equality

III.2.HS.2

33 Which amendment to the U.S. Constitution helped to correct the abuses highlighted in this document?

A First Amendment
B Fifth Amendment
C Fourteenth Amendment
D Nineteenth Amendment

III.3.HS.3

34 Which of the following U.S. Supreme Court cases dealt with an issue similar to the problem expressed in this document?

A *Marbury v. Madison*
B *McCulloch v. Maryland*
C *Brown v. Board of Education*
D *Gideon v. Wainwright*

III.3.HS.1

Civics

Directions: You should take about 5 minutes to examine the following graphic organizer and use it with what you already know to complete this task.

PROPOSAL 1:
The President of the United States shall serve only one six-year term.

PROPOSAL 2:
The electoral college system for electing the President shall be replaced with a system of direct election by the people.

PROPOSED CONSTITUTIONAL AMENDMENTS

PROPOSAL 3:
The President of the United States shall have the power of a line-item veto.

PROPOSAL 4:
There shall be a two-term limit for members of the U.S. Congress.

PROPOSAL 5:
Members of the U.S. Supreme Court shall serve for specified terms of 14 years rather than for life.

35 On the lines provided, select **two** of the proposed Constitutional amendments and explain why each would have either a favorable or unfavorable impact on the American political system.

Selection of first proposed amendment: _____

Explanation of how the amendment you selected would have either a favorable or unfavorable impact:

_____

_____

_____

_____

_____

Selection of second proposed amendment: _____

Explanation of how the amendment you selected would have either a favorable or unfavorable impact:

_____

_____

_____

_____

_____

III.4.HS.1

Name _____ Teacher _____

Economics

Directions: Read the following chart and use it with what you already know to answer the questions that follow.

HOW DEVELOPING NATIONS ATTEMPT
TO SOLVE THEIR ECONOMIC PROBLEMS

COUNTRY 1	The government has recently nationalized foreign-owned industries. It has spent large sums on the military and on public works projects — dams, roads, schools and factories.
COUNTRY 2	The government has decided to assist domestic agricultural production. To achieve this, it has instituted a high protective tariff on all agricultural imports.
COUNTRY 3	High birth rates and severe food shortages face this nation. The government has begun a program to limit birth rates by encouraging families to have no more than one child.
COUNTRY 4	The government has decided to allow foreign goods and investments to enter into the country with little interference. It hopes to encourage foreigners to invest in businesses in the country.

36 Which of these countries is MOST likely to have a free market economy?

A Country 1
B Country 2
C Country 3
D Country 4

IV.4.HS.5

37 What would MOST likely be a direct result of the actions taken by Country 2?

A An increased volume of foreign trade
B An increase in agricultural exports
C Strong opposition by farm workers
D A decrease in imported agricultural products

IV.4.HS.1

38 Which two countries are using their fiscal powers to help resolve some of their economic problems?

A Countries 1 and 2
B Countries 2 and 3
C Countries 1 and 3
D Countries 3 and 4

IV.3.HS.2

39 Which economic goal do all of these countries have in common?

A They are seeking to increase their economic growth.
B They want highly industrialized economies.
C They are trying to control foreign industries.
D They are driven by the desire to make profits.

IV.3.HS.3

40 The governments of China under Mao Zedong, Cuba under Fidel Castro, and the Soviet Union under Joseph Stalin followed polices most similar to those of which country?

A Country 1
B Country 2
C Country 3
D Country 4

IV.4.HS.5

Economics

Directions: Examine the following illustration and use it with what you already know to answer the questions that follow.

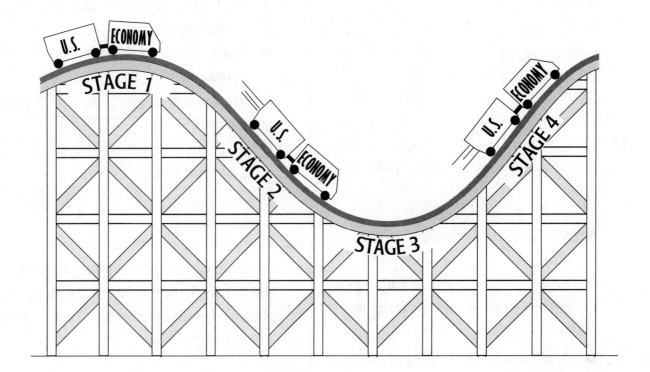

Economics

41 Which fiscal policy would the national government most likely institute if the economy was in Stage 3?

A Decrease taxes
B Cut government spending
C Increase taxes
D Raise interest rates

IV.3.HS.2

42 What monetary policy would the Federal Reserve System follow if the economy was in Stage 3?

A Increase taxes
B Increase interest rates
C Decrease interest rates
D Decrease government spending

IV.3.HS.2

43 Which policy would the federal government probably follow if it was worried that prices were rising too quickly in Stage 1?

A Decrease taxes and lower interest rates
B Increase tariff rates
C Raise interest rates
D Lower tariff rates

IV.3.HS.2

44 What is the government's main purpose in using its fiscal and monetary powers to intervene in Stages 1, 2, 3, and 4?

A Acting to protect business investments
B Providing public goods and services
C Encouraging fair trade
D Promoting economic stability

IV.4.HS.3

45 Which economic indicator would provide the government with the BEST general picture of the economy at Stage 3?

A Unemployment rate
B Total value of imported goods and services
C Rate of inflation
D Consumer Price Index

IV.3.HS.1

Economics

Directions: Examine the following diagrams and use them with what you already know to answer the questions that follow.

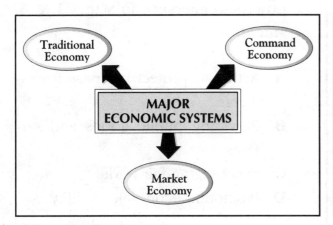

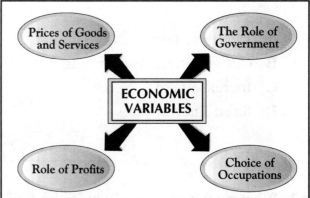

46 On the lines provided, select **two** economic variables and describe how one of the economic systems deals with that variable. You can use the same or a different economic system for each variable.

First variable selected: _____

How a_____ *(economic system you chose)* deals with that variable:

_____

_____

_____

Second variable selected: _____

How a_____ *(economic system you chose)* deals with that variable:

_____

_____

_____

IV.4.HS.5

Name _____ Teacher _____

Inquiry

Directions: You should take about 5 minutes to examine the following line graph and use it with what you already know to complete these tasks.

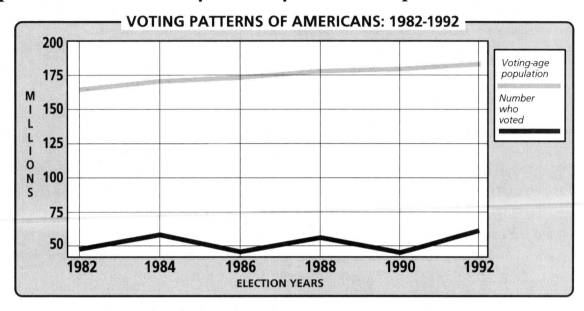

VOTING PATTERNS OF AMERICANS: 1982-1992

Task I:

47 Study the information in the line graph. Make a statement about the relationship between the **voting age population** and the **number of people who actually vote**. _____

_____

_____

Task II:

V.1.HS.3

48 Use the information in the graph to make a chart showing the voting patterns of Americans from 1982 to 1992. Be sure to label each category correctly.

Election Years		
1982		
1984		
1986		
1988		
1990		
1992		

V.1.HS.2

Name _____ Teacher _____

Inquiry and Decision-Making

Directions: Read the following information about a public policy issue. Use it with what you already know to complete the tasks that follow. You should take about 20 minutes to complete both Task I and Task II. Task I is a selected-response item and Task II is an extended-response item.

CAMPAIGN FINANCE REFORM

Americans are increasingly concerned about the way election campaigns are funded. One proposal Congress is considering is to ban contributions from *Political Action Committees* (PACs) and other organizations. PACs are committees formed by interest groups to funnel donations to political candidates who are likely to support them. The proposed reform would limit campaign spending to private individual contributions, government matching funds, and a candidate's own money. The following is some information that members of Congress are examining on this proposal:

DATA SECTION

PART A

A CHRONOLOGY OF MAJOR CAMPAIGN FINANCE LAWS AND COURT CASES

YEAR	LAW/COURT CASE	EFFECT
1947	**Taft-Hartley Act**	Prohibited direct campaign contributions to federal candidates from labor unions, corporations, and interstate banks.
1974	**Federal Election Campaign Act**	Placed limits on individual and group contributions to candidates and political parties; provided a system of government matching funds for qualified candidates.
1976	***Buckley v. Valeo***	The U.S. Supreme Court upheld limits on contributions to candidates and parties, but struck down limits on expenditures by candidates in their own campaigns.

Inquiry and Decision-Making

PART B

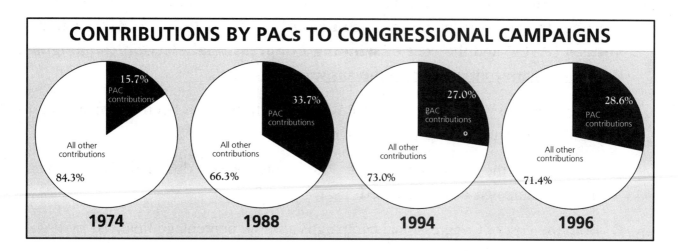

CONTRIBUTIONS BY PACs TO CONGRESSIONAL CAMPAIGNS

PART C

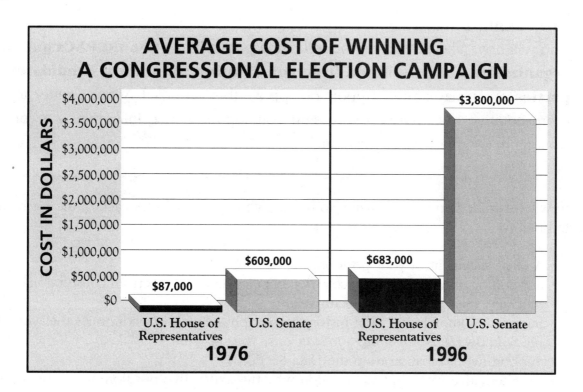

AVERAGE COST OF WINNING A CONGRESSIONAL ELECTION CAMPAIGN

Inquiry and Decision Making

COMPLETE THE FOLLOWING TASKS:

Task I: Interpreting Information

49 Study the information in the Data Section. Which of the following statements best describes the *relationship* between **contributions from Political Action Committees (PACs)** and the **cost of winning Congressional election campaigns**? <u>Be sure to mark your answer on the answer sheet.</u>

A In the past 20 years, increases in PAC contributions have been the main factor behind the dramatic rise in campaign costs.

B Since 1974, the dollar amount of PAC contributions declined slightly even though campaign costs increased.

C Both the cost of Congressional campaigns and the percentage financed by PACs have generally increased since 1974.

D Since 1974, non-PAC contributions to Congressional candidates have increased at a faster rate than PAC contributions.

Task II: Taking a Stand

50 You will now take a stand on the following public issue: **Should PACs and other organizations be prohibited from contributing to political candidates and parties?** You may either support or oppose this proposal. Write a letter to your representative in Congress expressing your opinion. Use information to provide reasons that support your position.

You will be graded on the following, so be sure your letter includes each of the elements listed below:

- A clear statement of your position.
- Supporting information using core democratic values of American constitutional democracy. (See page 146 for examples.)
- Supporting knowledge from history, geography, civics, or economics that you already know. *(It is not enough to state only your opinion.)*
- Supporting information from the Data Section.
- An alternative view and explanation why the alternative position would be a less effective public policy.

Inquiry and Decision Making

Remember to: Use complete sentences.
Explain your reasons in detail.
Write or print neatly on the lines provided.

Should PACs and other organizations be prohibited from contributing to political candidates and parties?

Dear Representative:

_____

_____

_____

_____

_____

_____

_____

_____

_____

_____

_____

_____

_____

continued...

Name _____   Teacher _____

196

_____

_____

_____

_____

_____

_____

_____

_____

_____

_____

_____

Use this checklist to review your letter.

- ❑ I stated my position clearly.
- ❑ I supported my position with reference to at least one core democratic value of American constitutional democracy.
- ❑ I supported my position with knowledge from history, geography, civics, or economics that I already knew.
- ❑ I supported my position with information from the Data Section.
- ❑ I stated an alternative view and explained why it would be a less effective public policy.

Name _____ Teacher _____

INDEX

ANSWER SHEET FOR SELECTED-RESPONSE QUESTIONS IN PRACTICE HIGH SCHOOL TEST IN SOCIAL STUDIES

Student_____ Class_____

Teacher_____ Date_____

DAY ONE

GEOGRAPHY					HISTORY			
1	Ⓐ	Ⓑ	Ⓒ	Ⓓ	12	Ⓐ	Ⓑ	Ⓒ	Ⓓ
2	Ⓐ	Ⓑ	Ⓒ	Ⓓ	13	Ⓐ	Ⓑ	Ⓒ	Ⓓ
3	Ⓐ	Ⓑ	Ⓒ	Ⓓ	14	Ⓐ	Ⓑ	Ⓒ	Ⓓ
4	Ⓐ	Ⓑ	Ⓒ	Ⓓ	15	Ⓐ	Ⓑ	Ⓒ	Ⓓ
5	Ⓐ	Ⓑ	Ⓒ	Ⓓ	16	Ⓐ	Ⓑ	Ⓒ	Ⓓ
6	Ⓐ	Ⓑ	Ⓒ	Ⓓ	17	Ⓐ	Ⓑ	Ⓒ	Ⓓ
7	Ⓐ	Ⓑ	Ⓒ	Ⓓ	18	Ⓐ	Ⓑ	Ⓒ	Ⓓ
8	Ⓐ	Ⓑ	Ⓒ	Ⓓ	19	Ⓐ	Ⓑ	Ⓒ	Ⓓ
9	Ⓐ	Ⓑ	Ⓒ	Ⓓ	20	Ⓐ	Ⓑ	Ⓒ	Ⓓ
10	Ⓐ	Ⓑ	Ⓒ	Ⓓ	21	Ⓐ	Ⓑ	Ⓒ	Ⓓ

INQUIRY AND DECISION MAKING

23 Ⓐ　　Ⓑ　　Ⓒ　　Ⓓ

DAY TWO

CIVICS					ECONOMICS			
25	Ⓐ	Ⓑ	Ⓒ	Ⓓ	36	Ⓐ	Ⓑ	Ⓒ	Ⓓ
26	Ⓐ	Ⓑ	Ⓒ	Ⓓ	37	Ⓐ	Ⓑ	Ⓒ	Ⓓ
27	Ⓐ	Ⓑ	Ⓒ	Ⓓ	38	Ⓐ	Ⓑ	Ⓒ	Ⓓ
28	Ⓐ	Ⓑ	Ⓒ	Ⓓ	39	Ⓐ	Ⓑ	Ⓒ	Ⓓ
29	Ⓐ	Ⓑ	Ⓒ	Ⓓ	40	Ⓐ	Ⓑ	Ⓒ	Ⓓ
30	Ⓐ	Ⓑ	Ⓒ	Ⓓ	41	Ⓐ	Ⓑ	Ⓒ	Ⓓ
31	Ⓐ	Ⓑ	Ⓒ	Ⓓ	42	Ⓐ	Ⓑ	Ⓒ	Ⓓ
32	Ⓐ	Ⓑ	Ⓒ	Ⓓ	43	Ⓐ	Ⓑ	Ⓒ	Ⓓ
33	Ⓐ	Ⓑ	Ⓒ	Ⓓ	44	Ⓐ	Ⓑ	Ⓒ	Ⓓ
34	Ⓐ	Ⓑ	Ⓒ	Ⓓ	45	Ⓐ	Ⓑ	Ⓒ	Ⓓ

INQUIRY AND DECISION MAKING

49 Ⓐ　　Ⓑ　　Ⓒ　　Ⓓ

NOTES